CHRISTIANITY IN INDIA

CHRISTIANITY IN INDIA

By

Arthur Mayhew

GYAN

Christianity in india

Arthur Mayhew

ISBN : 978-81-212-0143-8

First Published 1994, reprint 2013 in India by
Gyan Publishing House
23, Main Ansari Road, Daryaganj,
New Delhi - 110002
Phones : 23282060, 23261060

Fax : (011) 23285914
E-mail: books@gyanbooks.com
website: gyanbooks.com

Printed at : Sagar Color Scan, New Delhi.

CONTENTS

PART I—1600–1793

CONTENTS

PART II—1793–1813

CONTENTS

PART III—1813–1857

CONTENTS

EPILOGUE

PREFACE

CRITICS who reach the end of this book may detect in its later chapters a note more appropriate to the close of last century than to an age suspicious of all imperial pretensions. It is true that the facts which I have collected and examined have made clear to me what India owes to the Christian spirit that has in ever-increasing measure animated our administration of that country. But no attempt has been made to hide the fact that we are still very far from having discharged in full the obligation imposed by our public profession of the Christian faith. And the credit for an achievement, and still more for aims, unique in history, is assigned, not to the nation which has undertaken the task, but to the spiritual atmosphere and foundations of the society in which its representatives have been reared. Often unconsciously, and sometimes with protestations to the contrary, those responsible during the last century and a half for India's welfare have for the most part brought with them, not only as Mr. Kipling suggests the Law and the Prophets, but also the spirit of the Gospels. This statement may embarrass a bureaucracy unused to praise. It suggests visions of a Simla secretariat engaged under episcopal supervision in translating the Sermon on the Mount into official jargon. There may be secretaries who read the Bible during office hours. But they would resent being caught in the act.

Christianity in relation to Government does not imply official recognition of a system of ethics or the substitution of the Gospels for orders and regulations. Ultimately it means a conception of God's relation to men which impresses on rulers a sense of the value and dignity of every member and every class of society, and which inspires a belief in the possibility of human progress, because history and experience have revealed the presence of divine attributes in men. It means a progressive vigour which arises from consciousness of God's Spirit at work in the hearts and councils of men. It is a faith which is idealism in action, enabling even officials

'To hope till hope creates
From its own wreck the thing it contemplates.'

No one who compares carefully the British administration of India with its predecessors can fail to find in it this differentiating note of hopeful determination. If we call it a western note, it is only because it was to the West that the Roman Empire gave an opportunity of rebuilding its civilisation on the life and teaching of one who recognised no geographical distinctions. By undertaking a similar task for eastern peoples the British Empire has been reminded of the foundations on which all that is permanent and great in it is based.

Confronted in India with a civilisation that demands religious sanction for all its customs, regardless of their moral value, British rulers have been less inclined to ignore a religion which essentially can be identified only with what is highest in man's nature. To the Hindu philosopher all religions may be equally true; the administrator comparing a Christian settlement with the pariah village at its gates has good reason to know that they are not all equally effective. And he will note as more than a coincidence, the readiness of the religion which has been socially and morally most effective to submit its doctrines to the test of history and psychological experience.

Working under these conditions, as trustees for India, our representatives accepted without a protest the bold profession of the Christian faith imposed on them by

Queen Victoria. Men who at home would hesitate to proclaim adherence to any church have been ready, in surroundings that throw into bold relief the pragmatic excellence of Christianity, to claim, without any feeling of hypocrisy, its patronage for their activities. Our policy has been moulded by men who have come gradually to see that the distinction between Christian missionary and administrator in India is one of scope and method rather than of aims or motive power.

The earlier chapters are to some extent a record of failure and wasted opportunities, serving perhaps to chasten the feelings that the later portion is intended to evoke. The partial failure of those years was due to lack of courage, sincerity, and understanding of the peoples committed to our charge. India demands these gifts pre-eminently of her rulers.

It was my original intention to make this book a personal record of great men in the official and missionary worlds who attacked most vigorously the problems arising out of contact between Christian rulers and non-Christian peoples. But the personal note so easily maintained in the earlier chapters is lacking in the later parts. No figures, in fact, stand out with the impressive majesty of Schwartz and Carey, Lord Wellesley and John Lawrence. This implies no falling off in the spirit or quality of evangelical and administrative work. Increasing readiness on the part of Government to honour Christian obligations, educational progress, and gradual enlightenment of public opinion, have transformed prophets and pioneers into men distinguished by unobtrusive and impersonal activity, more anxious to gain colleagues than disciples. It is the mountain peaks that catch the first glow of dawn. But as day advances the valleys with their record of humble but fruitful co-operation are also a source of inspiration to the painter.

CHRISTIANITY AND GOVERNMENT OF INDIA

The influence of a Christian Government on the social, moral, and religious life of India is a large enough subject for one book. Subjects such as the opium and liquor trade, the treatment of Indians in our colonies, and the regulation of indentured labour have been omitted. They raise questions of moral and religious importance but they cannot be discussed without political and economic knowledge and insight to which I can make no claim. On all such subjects Christian-hearted students may differ from one another in their conclusions. I have dealt primarily with topics on which the Christian world is substantially agreed.

Aiming at a demonstration of the mutual relations existing between the Government and Christian missions I have had but little space for emphasising the importance of non-Christian workers who have exposed the nobler elements in Hinduism and Islam by their co-operation in the uplifting of their country. The significance of such co-operation has not been wholly ignored.

An attempt has been made to compare the general attitude of Hindu thought and feeling to social and moral problems with that of Christianity. To Islam inadequate space and attention have been devoted. I should be sorry if this were misconstrued as failure to realise the important part that this great religion will play in the development of India, when it has realised more fully the supreme importance of education. Educational shortcomings in the past have prevented it from rendering assistance worthy of its reputation, while its general characteristics have not imposed so many obstacles to reform as popular Hinduism has done. But even this does not wholly account for the few pages I have given it. Further study would have postponed completion of the book. An excuse that will appeal more to my readers is that it would have added substantially to its length.

PREFACE

For the past I have relied for facts almost entirely on the labours of others, whether in the shape of reports, histories, memoirs, or biographies. The list of my creditors will show the catholicity of my borrowing. I can claim no merit for independent research. Sometimes I have failed, and more often I have lacked time or opportunity, to verify facts or authorities quoted in the works I have consulted. But I have done my best in my borrowing to investigate the general character and reputation of my benefactors. I have formed my own conclusions, but they have often turned out to be those of others also. If I have failed anywhere to give credit where credit is due, the fault may charitably be ascribed to the fact that I have reflected so long over some statements that they have come to seem my own.

The book is patchwork. But patchwork can yield a new design and be serviceable. Many have written about Christian missions, and more about our rule in India. If I have helped to connect the two subjects, as I am sure they ought to be connected, I shall not wholly have failed.

PART ONE

1600—1793

PART I—1600–1793

CHAPTER I

WILBERFORCE AND THE CHARTER OF 1793

Carey's repulse—licenses for missionaries—struggle for right of entry—Wilberforce's aims and disappointment—the Company's attitude—its fears and difficulties—apathy of the Christian Churches.

ENGLAND in 1793 was anxious and perplexed. With the Bank of England suspending payment, Jacobins at work on either side of the Channel, and 'The Rights of Man[1]' spreading poison over the countryside, men's hearts were failing them for fear. No one who knew William Carey would have dared to accuse him of despair. But when that 'consecrated cobbler' and his co-mate in enthusiasm Thomas, late surgeon of the East India Company Fleet, watched from Plymouth Hoe the East Indiaman, which should have conveyed them and their Bibles to Bengal, hull down on the horizon, there can have been few more troubled minds in that troublous year. For Captain Smyth, who had yielded so far to the persuasive tongue of Thomas as to smuggle them on board at Gravesend, had capitulated at Plymouth to the stronger coercion of a pseudonymous letter. To embark a passenger for John Company's domain in India without a licence from that Company involved on discovery alarming penalties. But unlicensed passengers who were also 'missionaries and schoolmasters'! It was as much as his place was worth. So he had sailed without them.

[1] Published 1790. The author, Tom Paine, was prosecuted in 1792, and produced in France *The Age of Reason* in 1793.

Carey and Thomas, knowing Leadenhall Street[1] too well to knock again at those doors, were left to their own devices. 'Attempting great things for God' they confidently 'expected great things'. Not many months had passed before a friendly Danish East Indiaman, which had adopted them in their distress, played the part of an evangelical cuckoo and deposited them in an unsuspecting Company's nest

William Wilberforce too was not inclined to admit despair or defeat. But in this same year of grace, 1793, being the seventh after his conversion, his soul was sadly troubled and the serenity of the Clapham circle was marred. What did it profit that Sunday schools were arising on all sides, that Hannah More was bringing light to Mendip miners, that prison life was being transformed by Howard, or that lunatics and slaves were beginning to claim Christian attention? Yet another sin had been added to the national account for which the chastisement of Heaven must be awaited. The House of Commons, which had accepted the pious resolution that the time had come for securing the advancement of India in 'useful knowledge and religious and moral improvement', had refused to translate theory into practice, when it proceeded to revise the Charter of the East India Company and to consider definite measures for relieving the condition of their most distressful subjects. A clause reaffirming the accepted resolution, and specifically providing for the despatch of 'a sufficient number of schoolmasters and missionaries to be maintained by the Governments of the Presidencies', had been rejected. And it had been made sufficiently clear that the Directors were not going to be bullied or coaxed into promising licences for any missionary who applied. Without such licence a landing in their territories was

[1] Where East India House, headquarters of the East India Company, stood.

illegal. Summary expulsion followed discovery. Not long before, an expelled missionary, forced to work a passage home before the mast, had succumbed to his labours and disappointment. And here was William Carey separated by the salt estranging sea from the peoples he wished to serve ; and 'twenty millions committed to the providential protection of Brahma'![1] Small wonder that the Eclectic Society, from whose brains the Church Missionary Society was before long to spring fully armed, contented itself, 'till this tyranny be overpast' with discussing the best methods of propagating the Gospel in Botany Bay. India was apparently to be a close preserve for a Company that preferred managing the affairs of Juggernaut and taxing his devotees to the work of an evangelist.

It was indeed provoking. There was good reason for Wilberforce to lose some of his habitual sanity and humour. Sarcasm, exaggeration, even ignorance of the facts and functions of the Hindu gods, were to be expected of one who had, with no little encouragement, counted on so much and got so little. Leaving out of account the support of Archbishop More,[2] who had so bravely ignored the potential dangers of 'enthusiasm' in full blast, had he not rightly expected much from the seed so zealously sown in India by chaplains Brown and Buchanan ? Had not Chaplain Brown, one of the finest specimens of Simeon's vintage,[3] collaborated with Charles Grant, one of the Company's most esteemed servants, in a well thought out scheme for a Protestant mission to Bengal ? Even Cornwallis, the Governor General, though not visibly impressed, had at least 'raised no objections' to this scheme. Was not Cornwallis himself doing much

[1] Wilberforce's summary of the situation. (Coupland, *Wilberforce.*)
[2] Archbishop of Canterbury, 1783–1803.
[3] Charles Simeon, 1759–1836. Leader of Cambridge Evangelicals.

to purify and energise the Company's service as a whole, insisting on a more decent and respectable mode of life, though not yet persuaded that Sunday observance east of Suez was profitable or practicable? This scheme of Brown's had only recently been brought home by Charles Grant, who had spent the leisure of his voyage in describing for an English public the state of society among our Asiatic subjects in Bengal. His general conclusion was that in gratitude to India, if for no other reason, it was the Company's clear duty to put the means of grace more or less officially before those for whom they were responsible. These views, and the record of his spiritual life in India, had brought him into close touch with Clapham;[1] and it was Clapham plus Grant that had secured the nomination of Sir John Shore, one of their most blameless though not perhaps most effective associates, to the Governor-Generalship of India. Surely harvest time was at hand.

In less spiritual regions too there had been so much ground for hope. The Regulating Act of 1773 and Pitt's East India Act of 1784 had put an end to a 'State disguised as a merchant' and had brought an oligarchy, invested for the first time with definite responsibilities, under the general control of Parliament. And since 1760, in the affairs of Clive and Hastings, Parliament had shown unmistakably that England was beginning to view her colonies and dependencies not solely as a means to money-making, but with some pride of territory and race, and some sense of obligation. It was not merely that the returned Nabob, with his presumably ill gotten gains, his readiness to out-do in splendour established leaders of society, and his pecuniary influence in elections and votes, was beginning to involve the

[1] For description of the Clapham Circle and personalities of this group of sturdy evangelicals see Fitzjames Stephen's article in *Edinburgh Review*, vol. lxxx, 1844.

Company in suspicion. Moral indignation had also its part to play. In any scheme of conversion Burke had no interest. The 'dignity and opulence of its princes, its ancient and venerable priesthood' meant far too much for him. But his speeches on India had impressed on their hearers an idea of trusteeship which was certainly inconsistent with the exclusion of 'missionaries and schoolmasters'. If he had failed to convict Hastings, he had certainly ended a system which had made Hastings' lapses, if such they were, inevitable. That system under which 'Asiatics had no rights and Europeans had no obligations' was gone for ever. In the new Regulations for Bengal Cornwallis had emphasised unmistakably the new conception of Empire. And Company servants such as Grant, Chambers, Udney and Weston, were prepared to assert in theory and prove in practice that the ten commandments had no purely local application. But Grant and Wilberforce were too impetuous. 'No enthusiasm, gentlemen, please' may offend a diocesan meeting when heard from episcopal lips. But it was a sound motto for negotiations with the easily scared but not essentially evil Directors of John Company. They could easily be coaxed, as Grant found later when he joined their band. But they were not going to be driven. Moreover, by claiming direct Government support and patronage for missions, Clapham was demanding of men, who had only recently realised that responsibility cannot be shirked, what the Government of India after more than a hundred years of concentrated meditation on its duties could not possibly to-day be induced to admit. And it must be added that they were demanding what William Carey from the first moment of his landing in India disclaimed, what few missionaries since his day have suggested, and what would most certainly have robbed missionary work of much of its spiritual form and vitality.

It was no such consideration that led the Company to marshal its forces inside and outside Parliament for the rejection of the clause. Nor were they consciously animated by any scruples as to their right to impose alien beliefs on subjects committed to their charge. Some spirit of tolerance they may have had, of which there will be more to say hereafter. But when they gravely pronounced, as they did in this same year 1793, that 'the Hindus had as good a system of faith and morals as most people and it would be madness to attempt their conversion' they were merely making a specious tolerance serve as cover to their timidity.

'When we consider for how many centuries after Christ providence allowed the greater part of mankind to live and die without any possibility of their attaining to the knowledge of the sacred truths by any human exertion, we must be satisfied that the rapid and speedy conversion of the whole world forms no part of the scheme of its Almighty Governor, and that it can give no offence in His eyes if we do not desert our domestic duties and expose the lives and worldly happiness of multitudes of our fellow-countrymen to hazard in order to attempt their conversion.'[1] Here there is no question of tolerance. Only a somewhat novel and daring interpretation of the Gospel with a view to reconciling God and Mammon. Not that much reconciliation is needed; so anxious is Providence to keep on friendly terms with this world that truth, though sacred, is doled out in such a way as to avoid all risk.

It is easy to ridicule this distortion of the uncompromising words of Christ; subsequent events have proved what a closer study of Indian history might have revealed that it is easy to exaggerate the bigotry and

[1] From Sydney Smith's article in *Edinburgh Review*, April, 1808. Though subsequent to the year under discussion it summarises the sentiment responsible for the decision of this year.

religious scruples of the peoples of India. But the Directors were amazingly ignorant and they were in a difficult situation. They had to satisfy their shareholders as well as a Parliament whose concern for the moral and spiritual welfare of England was only intermittent. The careless intervals were too often devoted to a ruthless scrutiny of the Company's finances. In the good old days when the Company was in a position to relieve a harassed Government by a loan, its monopoly had been unchallenged. There had been no awkward talk of a trustee's duties. With a falling revenue, and a prospect of borrowing rather than lending, caution was surely justifiable.

'The Hindus', so their returned servants told them, 'were of all people the most capable of adopting desperate resolutions'[1] And the Mohammedans were even worse, as even Chaplain Kerr, when advocating support to the Society for the Promotion of Christian Knowledge, had admitted. With a tiresome devotion to their religion, they combined 'a climate and domestic habits' that restricted painfully 'the sale of broadcloth and hardware'. The Directors would be doing their duty neither to the shareholders nor the British nation if they allowed 'itinerant tinkers to preach the natives into insurrection'. Before all things discretion. 'The natives must be taught a better religion at a time and in a manner that will not inspire them with a passion for political change'. Let us, in fact, work to place our parents in affluence rather than a parcel of Hottentots in the way of salvation. Our duties to our families and country are set before us by God Himself. We are not at liberty to desert them in order to give a remote chance of conferring greater benefits on strangers at a distance'. The Eastern Empire in faot was not willingly

[1] This and following quotations are from an article in the *Edinburgh Review*, vol. xv, 1810, and from the 1808 article.

to be exposed to ruin for the conversion of half a dozen Brahmins.

Nor could Wilberforce turn confidently for support to the churches. Despite the benediction of Archbishop More, tne S.P.C.K., which had for some time been assisting the Danish mission in Calcutta and south India, was financially embarrassed, unable to obtain English volunteers, and in no position to press a forward policy. The General Assembly of the Kirk of Scotland was shortly to carry a resolution affirming that 'to spread abroad among barbarians and heathen natives the knowledge of the Gospel seems to be highly preposterous, in so far as it anticipates, nay even reverses, the order of Nature.'[1]

In other words England, and even Scotland, must convince the heathen that they have a religion before they try to spread it. 'Telescopic philanthropy' made no appeal to them. Mrs. Jellaby with her 'African project'[2] was still in her cradle. And the President of the Baptist Conference in 1786 had vainly tried to chasten the eager Carey, fresh from the construction of his map of heathendom. 'Sit down, young man. When it pleases the Lord to convert the Heathen, He will do it without your help or mine'. No one seemed in a hurry except Wilberforce and Carey; Wilberforce had to possess his soul in patience for another twenty years; Carey, before half that period had elapsed, had not only forced his way into Bengal, but had convinced its rulers that he was indispensable.

[1] In the year 1796.

[2] 'The African project involving her in correspondence with public bodies and private individuals anxious for the welfare of their species.' *Bleak House*, Dickens.

CHAPTER II

SCHWARTZ, THE EAST INDIA COMPANY AND OTHER EUROPEAN POWERS IN INDIA

Occasional friendliness of the Company to missions—Schwartz's career and services to the Company—The Danish mission and S.P.C.K.—their usefulness to the authorities in south India—S.P.C.K. in Bengal—the Directors' wariness—their evangelical aims in the seventeenth century—and subsequent coolness—attitude of Portuguese and Dutch authorities—the Danish mission and Tranquebar Government—Directors' non-committal attitude—due to indifference and fear—not tolerance—primarily concerned with dividends—evil reputation of Europeans and Christians in India—improvement in last quarter of eighteenth century.

We shall find Wilberforce in 1813 making full use of the tact and diplomacy of which he had no lack. It was ignorance rather than tactlessness which caused his failure in 1793 and the depression that followed. Had he not been preoccupied with his inadequate knowledge of Bengal, and ignorant of affairs in south India, he would have realised that the East India Company's bark was far worse than its bite. By a right instinct, though supported by argument that hardly wins respect, it had decisively refused to commit itself to any mission work. But for many years the Directors and their servants in India alike had been establishing the friendliest of relations with Christian missionaries, based on mutual service discreditable to neither side. Though they were not prepared to admit unquestioned any missionary who might desire their licence, they had already discovered the potential usefulness of the class as a whole, and had not hesitated to express in words and action their gratitude and even sympathy.

By its charter of 1698 the Company was in fact pledged to active support of evangelical projects. For in that year Parliament had insisted that the Company's chaplains 'should apply themselves to learn the languages of the countries, the better to enable them to instruct the Gentoos, who should be the servants of the Company or their agents, in the Protestant religion'. A few of the chaplains in Madras had loyally carried out their instructions, and more, with the definite approval of the Company, had supported the evangelists when the Danish mission or the S.P.C.K. brought them to their notice. What would Wilberforce have thought had he known that the Company, whose godless indifference had brought him so near despair, was going a few years later to erect a memorial in their Church of St. Mary in Fort St. George which still records their appreciation of the 'transcendent work' of Christian Friedrich Schwartz and their 'grateful sensibility of the public benefits which resulted from his influence'. When it suited their purpose they could listen to Montgomery Campbell traducing the career of this great missionary in his attack on the 1793 clause in the House of Commons. That was politics. And Campbell was very properly considering the '*amour propre*' of his uncle, the Governor of Fort St. George,[1] whose private secretary he had been. Schwartz's views on the correct treatment of the King of Tanjore had been in sharp conflict with those of the Governor. And Schwartz had won. But this did not deter the Directors from paying their open tribute to one 'in whom religion appeared not with a gloomy aspect or forbidding mien, but with a graceful form and placid dignity'. And their fear of native bigotry had not restrained them from sanctioning in 1771 an annual grant of 500 Pagodas for the work that

[1] Sir Archibald Campbell, Governor of Madras, 1786–1789.

Schwartz and his companions were doing in South India. This grant was still being paid regularly at the time when Wilberforce received his rude rebuff.

It was Schwartz pre-eminently who established in India the fact that 'Christian things done in a Christian way' could give offence to none. In the hearts of all alike, native Rajahs, civil and military officers of the Company, and the most hardened officers in their troops, he inspired not only love, but a conviction of his ability for useful service. 'He is', said Hyder Ali, 'a holy man who means no harm to my Government. Let him travel anywhere'. 'Let them send the Christian to me', was the request of Tuljaji, sorely harassed King of Tanjore, 'there's no deceit from him'. And his adopted son Saroboji, whom he would so gladly have entrusted to the guardianship of Schwartz, and who was in fact directed and supported for so many years by his advice and care, in writing to ask of the East India Company a memorial of his life and death to be set up in the Tanjore church, ended his letter with the cry, 'Oh, Gentlemen, that you were but able to send missionaries who should resemble the departed Schwartz!' Flaxman's memorial, representing the King's last visit to the dying man, can still be seen in Tanjore church. Under it are lines that testify to the love, if not the poetic skill, of their writer and end:

> 'May I, my father, be worthy of thee,
> Wisheth and prayeth Saroboji'.

Equally generous, though less naïve, is the European tribute. 'The knowledge and integrity of this irreproachable missionary', wrote Colonel Fullerton, 'have retrieved the character of the European from imputations of general depravity'. And William Chambers, civil servant of Madras, records with envying approval the apostolic simplicity of his 'plateful of rice, boiled after the fashion of the country with a few vegetables. This formed his daily meal, and the piece of native cloth dyed black formed the material of his dress for a year '.

Such was the man who landed in Danish Tranquebar in 1750 as the agent of the Danish mission which then had nearly fifty years of honourable history behind it. Like most of its other agents he was a German, owing his inspiration to the Pietists of Halle. For more than fifty years, and from 1762 in territories owned or influenced by the English East India Company, he worked as evangelist, Company chaplain, schoolmaster, diplomatist, and father confessor of Raja, civil servant and common soldier. He died a wealthy man, for he was in the pay of the Danish mission, the S.P.C.K. and the East India Company, and many were the presents from wealthy Indians and Europeans for his services. But there is no reason to suppose that he ever viewed his wealth as anything but a trust fund which, depleted by frequent endowments of schools and chapels, he left behind him for the prosecution of mission work. For marriage he had no time nor liking. The only unhappy moment in a life of sunshine occurred when news reached him that Anne Sophie Pappe, selected and despatched by the Halle college which in its zeal had misread its instructions, was waiting for him in Tranquebar. It was not her 'flighty conduct' on the ship, as reported by fellow-passengers, that made him retreat into the hinterland and deposit with the authorities an affidavit of his devotion to celibacy. He had a heart large enough for the flightiest of wives, but the people of south India were his family. So a gallant lieutenant of the Danish Company's army stepped into the breach. He was old and apparently a match for Anne. The incident closes with a prayer of thanksgiving by Schwartz's colleagues, whose gratitude did not include the payment of Anne's travelling expenses.

With this trouble behind him he establishes schools

and churches in Trichinopoly, Tanjore, and Palamcotta. In Trichinopoly his influence with a somewhat suspicious Nawab is such that a Christian chapel is erected in the heart of a fort that is till nominally under Mohammedan rule. In Palamcotta his kindly zeal inspires the civil and military officers to assist a Brahmin woman convert in the building of a church. Everywhere he accompanies the European troops in the field and preaches to them, as the Company's chaplain, in their headquarter stations. The Government of Fort St. George uses his services in negotiations with Hyder Ali and later with Tippu Sahib. At the Court of Tanjore, where the British resident, John Sullivan, induced the Company to give a grant for his foundation of four schools, he was constantly employed. For two years in fact he was virtually the British Resident in that troubled Court. His success there was assured from his first interview with Tuljaji in 1769. The introduction he owed to a friendly German captain, Berg, in command of the royal troops. There sat Schwartz in a chair, twelve feet away from the royal bed, which was suspended from the ceiling, so that Tuljaji, cross-legged on it, could swing himself as he listened. The blessing with which Schwartz began shocked the satellites. But 'he is a priest', said Tuljaji with a reassuring gesture. Some expressions which followed seemed to the King 'rather too lively', but he smiled and said, 'Go on'. Then followed the tale of the prodigal son, after which pastry was brought in, and Schwartz was not only allowed to say grace, but even asked to sing a hymn. 'I have never', said the King, 'heard such things from a European before'. 'Remember that you are my padre' was his final benediction. This royal appointment was no sinecure. Intercourse for many years failed to isolate the King from his Brahmin entourage. Constantine similarly situated might have wavered. But there was something of the Edict of Milan in the simple words, 'They are my people', with which the King received a petition from Schwartz's converts. And the royal grant to Danish mission work was still paid in 1808 when Tuljaji and his adopted son had been gathered to their fathers.

Schwartz's career established beyond all doubt the fact that John Company by 1793, in south India at all events, far from resenting mission work, was ready to give it open approval and support, provided that it was tactful and not inflammatory and that the Company's interests were thereby promoted. Whether some of these pioneers carried tact too far, more particularly in their attitude towards caste and in the management of their finances, is a question that will arise later. Whatever may be the answer, it cannot dull the lustre of Schwartz's life and work.

In many other ways, but with the same point of view, the Government of Fort St. George showed friendliness to Schwartz's predecessors and contemporaries and a readiness to use them. As early as 1710 the German Ziegenbalg, first Protestant missionary in India, an agent of the Danish mission at Tranquebar, was courteously received by the Madras authorities on the recommendation of their chaplain. 'No feeling', said the chaplain, 'will be aroused if we do not sound a trumpet before us'. In 1715 they sent a definite invitation to the Danish mission to open up work in their territories and at the same time they told the S.P.C.K. in England, which had already begun to assist the mission, that they were 'ready on all occasions to patronise and encourage that noble and useful design'. Their pathetic request for *English* missionaries was beyond the spiritual capacity of England under George I. In 1735 Schwartz, firmly established as S.P.C.K. agent in Madras, was helped by the Government to open a native school. His successor, Fabricius, scholar, lexicographer, and unfortunately speculator, was given by the Government a church that had belonged to a Roman Catholic community, found wanting at the time of the French occupation. With similar encouragement but less success, owing to French excursions and alarms and Hyder Ali, work was started in Cuddalore and Negapatam. Even in the extreme south, beyond Schwartz's area of Tanjore and Trichinopoly, Gericke planted a mission which, in spite of occasional protests from the Company's servants against the dangers of conversion, was receiving at the close of the eighteenth century very friendly treatment and protection at the hands of the magistrates. By 1772 German and Danish missionaries were ministering to 2,200 converts in the Tamil territories of the Company, and were openly preferring their nominally 'un-privileged' position there to their treatment by the Danish authorities in an area where they enjoyed the King of Denmark's patronage.

Characteristically the Company's representatives in south India laid down no principles and committed themselves finally to no policy. Where either party had anything to give, the other party was only too ready to receive and give a *quid pro quo*. Gericke in 1782 saved seven English officers from the ruthless Hyder Ali. His son was given a cadetship in the military establishment. Fabricius was allowed a 'Pipe of Madeira' at the price usually charged to the Company's servants, and invested forty pounds accordingly just in time before his financial crash. Their services as chaplains were freely used in the lean years when the Company's finances prevented all increase to the establishment and left many posts long unfilled. In 1785 some stranded and officerless troops at Chingleput accepted gladly the ministrations of the ubiquitous Gericke. As political agents, translators, interpreters, and information bureaux, they proved their worth. And the Company was not above borrowing money from them and giving them funds to invest. For many of these versatile philanthropists speculated with their mission funds; there were two conspicuous smashes, but for the most part they seem to have been well advised. In return the Madras authorities prevailed on the Directors to give free passages to many of the missionaries and free transport for heir letters and stores. To oblige those who had shown proof of tactful friendliness seemed to Leadenhall Street sound business. Licenses to all who asked, and official patronage under compulsion from Parliament, were a very different matter.

In Bombay there was no question of missionaries during the eighteenth century. Bengal had not had the same reason as Madras to recognise their uses. But they were not unknown there. A year after Plassey, Clive, who had been married by Fabricius in Madras, offered to Kiernander, the Danish mission agent who had been driven from Cuddalore by the French, protection, a house rent free, and ground for a church. In this church for thirty years he ministered to a very slowly growing congregation of native converts and to Europeans such as Grant and Udney, who were attracted more perhaps by his genial humanity than his piety. By marriage and investment he acquired wealth which he lost by imprudence at the age of seventy-eight. Eleven years of poverty and real humbleness of heart in Dutch territory closed his life. But church and congregation were sustained by Chaplains Brown and Buchanan who had by this time brought Simeon's flaming torch to India. Kiernander and two Germans who followed him received rather faint-hearted support from the S.P.C.K. In 1789 that Society netted its first real live Englishman. It is regrettable that the first English Protestant missionary in India proved before long a hopeless failure. The mission in that year was reported to be in a piteous state and the S.P.C.K. had neither funds nor men for setting it right. Even Lady Coote's ineffable condescension in attending a service in the Mission Church failed to restore vitality. For three years the missionaries tried in vain to establish a mission. What happened to Chaplain Brown's scheme for a Protestant mission under Government patronage has already been told. It was the darkest hour before the dawn. Surgeon Thomas had already detected and enrolled the genius of Carey. Four years after Kiernander's fall he was in Bengal.

Apart from Clive's initial invitation and the friendly interest of Grant and Chaplain Brown there are few signs of helpfulness on the part of the Bengal authorities. From a Calcutta such as William Hickey[1] sets before us one would expect no enthusiasm for the spreading of the Gospel. But it is equally true that there was no opposition or persecution. That the mission was ignored was due to the absence of a Schwartz or a Gericke, with positive virtues likely to endear them to a perplexed Government. There is no reason to suppose that any of the S.P.C.K. agents, whose study of the language or the habits of the princes or people had placed valuable information at their disposal, would have escaped the notice of Hastings or Cornwallis. Nor was their piety and devotion sufficiently manifest to make up, in official eyes, for their shortcomings. If Ringeltaube[2] was ever mentioned in Fort William the ideas associated with his name must have been far different from those connected with Schwartz's in Fort St. George .

At home during the century the Directors viewed with equal complacency the indifference of Bengal and the comparatively enthusiastic attitude of Madras towards the spiritual welfare of the natives. With unusual

[1] See his *Memoirs*. Hurst and Blackett.

[2] A representative of the S.P.C.K. in India whose shortcomings provided fuel for the *Edinburgh Review* attacks.

fervour and customary stateliness they had acknowledged in 1712 news of the reception of Ziegenbalg in Madras. 'We recommend you to give your countenance and protection to Protestant missionaries and do whatever you think proper for the strengthening of their hands in this difficult and honourable work of spreading the Gospel among the heathen'. But they sent no such instructions at any time to Bengal; and they recorded with discreet absence of comment a suggestion from the S.P.C.K. that 'preference shall be given to those whom the missionaries shall instruct'.

In the seventeenth century discretion had been less marked. It must have been an impressive spectacle in 1614, when the Lord Mayor of London and Directors of the Company attended the baptism at Poplar of a young Indian, brought home by an East Indiaman captain and educated by the Company, 'to be an instrument in converting some of his nation'. King James I chose for him the name of Peter with unusual self-effacement. And the preacher presented him as 'the first fruit of India'. We hear no more of Peter, but three years later the conversion of 'a Mohammedan atheist' is reported from Surat. In 1657 the Directors applied to Oxford and Cambridge for a chaplain, 'the Company having resolved to endeavour the advance and spreading of the Gospel in India'. A further spasm is marked by the Company's orders in 1670, that its Negro slaves are to be instructed in Christian principles and then freed. After this there is ominous silence till 1698 when they accepted without protest or, apparently, action the clause in their charter relating to the linguistic attainments and evangelical functions of their chaplains which has been recorded above. In the same year a prayer was drawn up for the Company which included the words 'that, we adorning the Gospel of our Saviour in all things, these Indian natives among whom we dwell, beholding our good works, may be won over'. And in 1750 a similar prayer was still in use. Both prayers suggest the frank abandonment of the original idea of active proselytising. Indeed, by 1662, with the settlement in Bombay the principle of toleration, which was later to harden into uncompromising neutrality, had been established. 'There shall be no compulsory conversion, no interference with native habits, and no cow-killing in Hindu quarters.'

It is easy in these days to overlook the historical importance of this order. That it was inspired by prudential and commercial, rather than by spiritual or ethical motives, is probable. None the less it marks a new era in the relations of the European powers to the heathen world. Of these relations generally there will be something to be said later. Meanwhile a comparison of Portuguese and English methods will be instructive.

Albuquerque, anticipating William Bentinck by three hundred years, was bold enough to prohibit suttee within Portuguese India in 1510. Equal resolution was shown from a very early date in advancing positively what was then thought to be the Gospel of Christ. It is true that Francis Xavier for a time tried to work, as Francis of Assisi had proposed three hundred years before, without the assistance of the secular arm. But in 1542, thoroughly disheartened, he had been forced to call on John III of Portugal for aid. This inaugurated a period, not perhaps of forcible conversion, but of very distinct pressure. Hindus were too useful to be suppressed, but the choicest posts in Government service as well as exemption from naval service were promised to converts, who also received free rice from the Treasury as a mark of official approval. Political and religious expansion was assisted by a state subsidy for mixed marriages. Mohammedans were treated with less consideration and would undoubtedly have been suppressed if the State could have had its way. The Inquisition, which found its way to Goa in 1546 was perhaps more concerned with heretics than infidels; but it prohibited definitely the practice of pagan rights, interpreting skilfully the King's guarantee of liberty of conscience as giving to natives permission only to live in their own faith. If they practised its ceremonies they were liable to punishment. And such punishment was not seldom inflicted, though the extreme penalty was invariably commuted to imprisonment, corporal correction, or the galleys.

In the Dutch East Indies under a Protestant power somewhat similar though not such drastic methods were employed. The principle of state assistance in the propagation of religion was frankly accepted in Ceylon from 1642 when the Dutch occupied that island. The erection of temples and pagan pilgrimages was forbidden, government appointments were reserved for Christians and non-attendance at religious schools treated as a State offence. By 1685, 320,000 Cingalese had yielded to these methods. A few years after we took over the island in 1800 almost all Tamil and Cingalese converts, inherited from the Dutch, had faded away.

It is unnecessary in these days to spend time over condemning such methods, but we may justly congratulate ourselves on the good sense of John Company in refusing from its earliest days to countenance any kind of pressure, and on the wisdom of the missionaries in our territories who abstained from advocating them. That Wilberforce and Grant in 1793 had any such methods in view is of course inconceivable. But Government patronage in India easily passes into Government pressure. Southey, in fact, a few years later, definitely advocated in the *Quarterly Review* a policy of bribes.[1]

[1] Vol. i, May, 1809. See p. 95 below.

And pressure or bribery in the eighteenth century, whatever might have been the intentions of Government, would inevitably have degenerated into persecution.

For once in a way prudential considerations harmonised with the spirit of the Gospel. But what the Company might have learned, and failed to learn, from the procedure in Portuguese and Dutch dominions was the general readiness of the Indian peoples to submit to the powers that be. There were in Portuguese or Dutch India no uprisings comparable to the Indian Mutiny. That mutiny, as we shall have cause to see, was due rather to uncertainty as to the real aims of Government than to any belief that a direct assault was being made on indigenous faiths or ceremonies. The fifty years of our rule in India that followed the decision of 1793 are marked by a timid shrinking from the political consequences of an open profession of the Christian faith, for which the story of the Portuguese and Dutch Indies provides no justification.

In the Danish settlement of Tranquebar we find an attitude towards the spread of Christianity that resembles more closely the policy, or its absence, of the East India Company. But there is this important difference that the Danish mission enjoyed the direct and official patronage of the Danish Court. At the outset of their work, on the other hand, they encountered on Indian soil far more bitter opposition, and even active persecution, from the Danish officials than was ever faced by missionaries on British territories. It may be that oppression and injustice were more flagrant on Danish than on British soil, or that the missionaries were more persistent and aggressive in their denunciation of it. But the evidence for this is slight.

It is generally assumed that Ziegenbalg and Plütschau, who landed in Tranquebar in 1705 with a charter from King Frederick IV of Denmark, were the first Protestant missionaries in India. One would like to believe that Pastor Worm who preceded them in 1620 could claim this honour. He was a Court chaplain of a satirical turn of mind whose references to the royal bastards, and other literary indiscretions, led to his being landed on the Coromandel coast bereft of three fingers and the royal favour. His misfortunes did not prevent him from directing the choir in the Company's devotions. And he may have begun the first translation of the Bible into an Indian tongue. His epithet, still to be seen in Tranquebar, only tells us that 'after much edifying work among the natives, not burned by the heat of the sun, but naturally and very happily, he was received by Christ into the heavenly kingdom'.

His previous record in any case was not such as to win him Court patronage, and his ministry does not seem to have won for him the crown of martyrdom. Both honours were reserved for Ziegenbalg, a German follower of the Pietist Franke of Halle, introduced to Frederick IV by the Royal chaplain who was also of that school. In the instructions which the King's evangelists took with them to India they were warned 'not to forget daily to pray that God would grant to our Royal House the reward of this pious work with every needful blessing for this life and the life to come'. Fortified by these instructions, Ziegenbalg and Plütschau devoted to meditation on the divine wisdom the next few months which they spent in the East Indiaman with the appropriate name of Sophia.

Their reception in Tranquebar was chilly. For long they were denied a shelter. But quite cheerfully they studied the Acts of the Apostles in the open square. Not long after we hear of Ziegenbalg being torn away from his Tamil translation of the Bible and his conveyance in dressing gown and slippers to the common jail. Here he was kept for four months without a trial. There was some vague talk of importunity in pleading for an oppressed widow. However, his new year's greeting to the Governor was so full of Christian love that he received in return the loan of paper and pencil which enabled him to proceed with his translation. One gathers from his records that his saintliness was, like all real saintliness, disarming and irresistible. When the Governor threatened extreme measures 'I too', he replied, 'will proceed—to extremes of love'. Such an attitude, combined with Christian tact and a capacity, shared by so many of his successors, for making himself useful, brought about a reconciliation in the end. The King's wishes received attention and his allowance of 2,000 Thalers was regularly paid. In 1756 the Danish Government sent officially some of the mission's agents to evangelise the Nicobar Islands. But the subsequent growth of rationalism in Germany and Denmark led to a decline in home support. And it must be added that there were black sheep among the missionaries who were responsible for the loss of local esteem. There was a genial representative who lived up to his name of Früchtennichts. The government allowance was paid up till 1808, when it was continued by the British East India Company, into whose hands the settlement for a time came. But spiritual vitality had been lost. And all alike agreed that from 1750 onwards these Danish missionaries did better work and received more generous official support under John Company than in lands where the royal instructions of Denmark carried weight.

Our enquiries so far have suggested that the position accepted, we should hesitate to say adopted, at the close of the eighteenth century by the East India Company and their local agents in their dealings with Christian missionaries was one of non-committal. Though by no means unfriendly or unaware of their potential usefulness, and though ready to take advantage of their services and reward them, they shrank from any open display of favour which might give the impression of definite and official patronage. They felt themselves under no obligation to risk their dividends or position by any steps that might lead to tumult or uprising, or to any radical changes in the habits and attitude of the peoples from whom their wealth was derived. Though definitely invested since 1773 with the responsibilities of a trustee and the furtherance of India's welfare, they were not prepared to go nearly so far as the Portuguese or Dutch, and not quite so far as the Court of Denmark, in taking what most of the Directors and their servants at that time must have considered to be the first and most essential steps for the moral and spiritual improvement of their subjects.

In estimating the responsibility of the Company we must be careful not to credit or debit them with ideas of modern growth. Their abstention from active interference in religion was due neither to theories of tolerance, as has already been noted, nor to any conviction that the Church lost by direct association with the State. In eighteenth-century England there was no well-marked line between things spiritual and temporal. The Church was very definitely a department of the State. The general atmosphere is familiar to students of the Roman Empire. Nor, despite the growth of rationalism during the century, is it permissible to suppose that, in theory anyhow, the majority of Directors or their servants found any comforting prospect of ultimate salvation or moral and spiritual improvement during their life outside the doctrines of the Christian Church. But this is all in the realm of theory. And however great the difference may be between eighteenth and twentieth-century theories, the two centuries are perhaps alike in this ; where Englishmen anyhow are concerned, human nature does not allow any Government, or in fact any body of men, to let theory have its way, when it is opposed to material interests or the dictates of what is called common sense. An East India Company Director, if driven into a corner by Wilberforce or Simeon, would probably have emerged, battered but still himself, with the conviction that, though undoubtedly the Christian faith, and that alone, was necessary for salvation, the Gentoos in actual fact were not much further from Christianity than many nominal Christians he knew. And anyhow his duty was first and foremost to the Company. As little injustice and as much moral improvement as possible by all means. But what he as Director got out of India was more important than what he gave to it. 'In fact, sir, with more than half the population of London gin-sodden and illiterate, what have we got to give India?' The answer, as the General Assembly of the Scottish Kirk had found, was difficult. Let us avoid at all costs 'preposterous benevolence'.

That India, up to 1780 at all events, demoralised those who worked there cannot be denied by anyone who has studied the memoirs of that period. To assume that the Englishman in India was ever very much inferior morally to his stay at home brothers would be unjust. But the days when the journey to and fro was an affair of months, not days, when leave was unknown, when the chances of return were 70 to 1 against, when concentration on sordid and material ends led to the accumulation of wealth that would enable one to exchange for ever the heat and disease of Calcutta for the amenities of Bath, and when few English women of unblemished character were present to lift society by their influence, were not days when one could expect the blameless life of an Anglo-Indian headquarters station of to-day. Public opinion in England was not manifestly on the side of righteousness. Public opinion in India fell short of even the English standard because there was not the same feeling for convention and respectability. That came very seldom east of Suez. Whether the ten commandments dominated the West may be answered by those who best knew eighteenth-century England.

Never at any time was there any open flouting of religion. In the first half of the seventeenth century of course religion was, even to the roughest of the merchant adventurers, a very real thing. The instructions for the very first voyage included provisions to be made for 'prayers every morning and evening in every ship', the whole company 'being called there unto with diligent eyes that none be wanting'. To the Purser, Bible and Book of Common Prayer were entrusted with the ship's stores. From 1607 a regular though not generous provision of chaplains was made. Many orders issued against ungodly living and in support of regular prayers. Fines for non-attendance were frequent. Presidents and Governors such as Oxenden, Aungier and Streynsham Master were characterised by very deep and genuine piety. The news received in 1671 that John Newton had become a Moor was received with surprise and regret. Urgent requests for consignments of stout and wine were frequently preceded by a demand for 'orthodox ministers'.

But even in the seventeenth century men's minds were preoccupied with the accumulation of wealth. The Company had been eighty years in India before they had time to think of church building. In 1669 a Deputy-Governor of Bombay had to be censured for holding drinking parties during church hours. A few years later Chaplin Evans[1] succeeded by private trade in amassing a fortune which enabled him on his return home to assume a position and lead a life which brought him to the See of Bangor. Job Charnock, struggling

[1] Chaplain of Fort St. George, 1692; traded in various parts of India; Bishop of Bangor, 1702; Meath, 1716.

with malaria in the fever swamps of the Hoogly, with an eye that foresaw the future greatness of Kalighat, was a greater man than Chaplain Evans who preferred speculation in Madras to his proper post at the side of this founder of Calcutta. And if Charnock sacrificed a cock yearly on the tomb of his black wife, as tradition tells us, there was a greatness and sincerity about him which does not mark the normal chaplains of that age. It was a sincerity that must have seen through the snuffling retort of the Directors to Charnock's account of one of his greatest feats. 'It was not your wit or contrivance, but God Almighty's good Providence' they wrote, 'which hath always superintended the affairs of the Company'. If this was really their opinion, their failure to add any chaplain to the establishment between the years 1760 and 1800, when the number of their European servants was growing so rapidly, is difficult to understand. Perhaps Chaplain Evans had shattered their faith in an ecclesiastical establishment.

The age was beginning in which England's name was most dishonoured in India. The Roman Catholic mission sent by the Portuguese to the Mogul Court with political designs had been perhaps responsible for the Indian conception of Christianity quoted by the chaplains to Sir Thomas Roe's embassy. 'Christian religion devil religion : Christians much drink, much do wrong, much beat, much abuse others'. But in the middle fifty years of the eighteenth century the Company's agents did very little to correct this estimate. India during these years had little to contemplate, as Burke reminds us, except 'an endless, hopeless prospect of new flights of birds of prey and passage, with appetite constantly renewing for a food that is continually wasting. Their prey is lodged in England and the cries of India are given to the sea and the winds.' William Hickey's *Memoirs* and the files of Hickey's *Gazette*, with its scandal and sordid small talk,[1] reveal the spirit of Calcutta, and the chronicles of Fort St. George are hardly more illustrious. The domestic life is summarised in a vivid picture of 'black wives running about picking up a little rice while their husbands please them by worshipping their favourite idol'.

'Empires cannot be built up in contempt of the laws of God and then be maintained according to the Decalogue . . . when the pedestals of the throne are terror and admiration, he who would sit there securely must consult other rules than those of the Evangelist. . . . The British administrator who shall be true to his employers and strictly equitable to the princes of India and their subjects need not despair of squaring the circle'.[2] In these gloomy words Fitzjames Stephen accounts for the failure of Sir John Shore (Lord Teignmouth) to accomplish anything of note in India, despite of, perhaps because of, his connections with the Clapham sect. Sir John Shore became Governor-General at the close of our blackest period in India, when it was becoming doubtful whether we could produce there anything great except military leaders. But stouter hearts than his, and abler brains, were shortly to proceed to the purging of our rule. Wilberforce's despair in 1793 was due perhaps less to the actual rejection of his clause than to the reports on Anglo-Indian society and Company's methods that Shore sent to the Clapham circle. He would have been more hopeful if he had foreseen what Cornwallis and Wellesley were to accomplish during the next fifteen years. The Bengal Regulations of Cornwallis indicated a new spirit of administration, and ideals such as those which Burke so long had advocated. Decency and discipline were instilled into the outward lives at least of the headquarters officials. Church-

[1] The first English paper published regularly in India, 1780.
[2] *Edinburgh Review*, vol. lxxx, 1844.

going again became fashionable, the cue of Lord Cornwallis being quickly followed. Chaplains Brown and Buchanan atoned for all the shortcomings of their predecessors. Grant and Chambers and other high officials set an example of godly living. There was even some talk of the closing of government offices and factories on Sunday; but this was more than even Cornwallis could attempt. 'Business as usual, but no horse-racing' was for the next few decades to be the watchword for Sunday. So much had affairs changed that within five years of the 'godless' rejection of Wilberforce's laws, the Directors, agitated regarding the condition of a church-building in Madras, reminded their agents there that they would 'preserve the ascendancy which our national character has acquired over the minds of the natives of India neither by disregard of the external observances of religion nor by any assimilation to Eastern manners or opinions, but rather by retaining the distinctions of our national principles, character, and usages'. Wise council, indeed, on which Lord Wellesley was shortly to take vigorous action. But it looked to the future not to the past. There was little in the Company's actions that had led the people of India to support any sinister designs of foisting an alien religion on them. There was much, in omission as well as commission, that had made them wonder whether the Company had any religion of their own to communicate.

CHAPTER III

PUBLIC OPINION IN CHURCH AND STATE AT HOME

General attitude to missions in seventeenth and eighteenth centuries—and to religion generally—significance of national and 'established' Churches—effect of Reformation on mission work—restrictions compared with wide scope of pre-Reformation Catholicism—foundation of S.P.C.K. and S.P.G.—eighteenth century mistrust of enthusiasm—signs of dawn—Evangelical revival.

But if the Company had its own reasons for refusing to let religion obtrude on the work and lives of their servants in the eighteenth century, what is to be said of the attitude of the English people, or of the oligarchy that they allowed to govern them in the eighteenth century? The ultimate responsibility of the Government for the welfare of the Indian peoples entrusted by them to the Company's charge was, as we have seen, fully admitted in the latter half of that century. How was it that the claims of a religion which was frankly recognised at home as necessary for the stability of the realm, and even, if judiciously administered, for its material advancement, received such slight attention where the progress of India was concerned?

It had not always been so. Up till the end of the seventeenth century there was a general recognition that plantations and colonising agencies were responsible for the propagation as well as the upkeep of religion. The instructions of Edward VI to navigators, that 'the service of Christianity must be the chief interest of such as shall make any attempt at foreign discovery', were for many years borne in mind, though they were never emphatically endorsed in action. The avowed object of Sir Humphrey Gilbert's scheme was 'The honour of God and compassion of poor infidels led captive by the Devil'. Walter Raleigh by his donation of £100 to the Virginia Company for propagation work headed the list of Protestant Mission contributions in England. The Charter of James I to the same company, and of Charles I to the Massachusetts Company, were as mindful of religious claims as the royal instructions to Spanish and Portuguese employers. The Long Parliament in 1647 resolved that 'it is our duty to assist the Heathen in New England who are beginning to call upon the Lord', and ordered a collection in all churches which raised £600 for John Eliot's work among the Red Indians. The Restoration Parliament in sanctioning the Prayer Book of 1662 must have been reminded of national obligations by the new prayer which remembered 'All sorts and conditions of men', and called for the communication of 'Thy saving help unto all nations'. The chaplain clause in the East Indian Company's charter of 1698, which has already been noted, was another mark of parliamentary interest in the subject.

But for the major portion of those who 'counted' in the eighteenth century the religion accepted by the state and society as a convenience was something to be used with tact and discretion at home. There was no need to diffuse it recklessly abroad. The general atmosphere, as has often been pointed out, was remarkably like that of Augustan Rome. To the statesman, thinking imperially, all religions were equally useful, each in its proper place. At home the Established Church must at all costs retain its position and privileges as a state department. Unitarians were outside the Toleration Act; the expenditure of a few thousand pounds on new church buildings, to counteract dangerous anti-social and levelling tendencies in the lower classes, was a sound investment. Lord Chesterfield thought it well to remind his son that clergymen have a useful part to play in society ; it was a vulgar error to suppose that all were necessarily hypocrites. And Christian apologetics, as expounded for instance in Queen Caroline's drawing-room, were a very elegant pastime.

But why should India not have its own established church or even churches ? They were strange peoples in the East, not perhaps fitted for the sturdy commonsense and nicely calculated probabilities of English divines. Infidels and papists could not of course be allowed openly to attack the fabric of church and state at home. There must be penal laws for them, just as there must be a denial of privileges to dissent. But an infidel in England might well be a pillar of the church in India. So a member of the council of Fort St. George argued when the anguish of a native Christian convert, who had lost his rights of inheritance by renunciation of his racial religion, was reported to him. 'You must remember', he replied, 'that in England we treat a Roman Catholic pervert with similar harshness'.

'Cujus regio eius religio' was a legacy from the Reformation. When away from Rome do what the provincial does and likes. It makes for stability. A Roman general set up an altar in north Africa to a local god who dominated the region where his troops had been victorious. Why should not John Company assume the management and undertake the protection of the temples, attendance at which presumably gave their frequenters the religious tone which social stability demanded ?

And the Church in England was still too much under the disintegrating influence of the Reformation to be able to attack effectively this local and particularising view of religion. The solidarity of Christendom had for a time been shattered by the sixteenth-century wave of nationalism. If Europe at the close of that century had been what the Holy Roman Empire was at the close of the dark ages there would have been few in India to-day who did not profess and call themselves Christians. That India would spiritually have been more advanced is an arguable point. But civilisation in the western sense of that term would have made more rapid progress.

When Augustine, with reckless misapplication of context, urged the temporal power to 'compel them to come in', he was dreaming of a world state, which in its two aspects, spiritual and temporal, would be a 'Civitas Dei'. After Charles Martel, Charlemagne, dukes of Poland and Teutonic knights, had carried out very literally for a few centuries this doctrine of compulsion, the European world had perhaps become 'so effectively inoculated with a very diluted and attenuated serum of Christianity that it was proof against violent attacks'. It may be that Christianity in its efforts to save the world and civilisation had come near to losing its own soul. It had to pay for assuming the position and methods of the Roman Empire. But we are all too apt to underrate the stabilising and civilising effect of the consolidated forces of the Christian world; there was a vital energy in it which kept the less virile, though not less brilliant, forces of the Caliphate out of Europe. The Crusades may have had their commercial side, but the Crusaders had the power of Christian Europe behind them. So did Vasco da Gama and Columbus and the Jesuits who established their reign of civilisation in Paraguay. But they were a survival. By the time Don John of Austria set out on the last of the Crusades 'The cold Queen of England was looking in the glass' and there was good cause for the Sultan of Byzantium to sit 'smiling in the sun'.

For seven centuries the conviction of a divine commission had given the European rulers a dignity and courage that impressed the peoples on her borders, and a strength that commanded respect. 'Overflowing with soft mastery, melting and embosoming, absorbing and absorbed, up came the subtle water everywhere, bathing the world. Invisible nets, impalpable soothing tendrils crept over human souls unconscious and delighted '.[1] 'The Church had gained a thousand selves by losing one. Her heavenly wishes, her awful sweetness, her iron endearments, the sympathy which earth cannot escape from though she would', had played their part. Europe socially and politically was saved. But spiritually the Church was exhausted. The new life which came to her in the latter half of the sixteenth century assumed a sectarian and national form. And many years were to elapse before the Protestant Churches were to remember that they had for the world a message which their fight for national independence had led them to forget.

The establishment of the Society for the Promotion of Christian Knowledge in 1698 was a sign that its Anglican founders, headed by Thomas Bray, had remembered that their responsibility as Churchmen was not confined to England. Their activities were not wholly extra-territorial. At an early meeting in 1700 sanction was given for the distribution of '800 copies of kind cautions against Swearing to the Hackney Coach men of London'. Superfluous copies were assigned at a later meeting to British seamen. But in 1709 Prince George's Danish chaplain called them to a more distant, though not perhaps more arduous, field. The Danish Mission in Tranquebar was already in difficulties. The S.P.C.K. joyfully dispatched to them a printing press and printer for the publication of Portuguese tracts against papistry in India. The press survived capture

[1] J. B. Mozley, *Essays in History and Theology.*

by a French privateer. And the good work led to regular financial contributions from the Society for a more Christian campaign against the whole heathen world. Ziegenbalg by the kind offices of the Society was invited to preach before King George I. By 1740 the Society was financially responsible for the mission's work in south India. The Archbishop of Canterbury condescended to inform Ziegenbalg that his lot was far higher than that of church dignitaries and that he would shine like the sun among the stars for ever. But this reckless concession to enthusiasm was not very fruitful. By the close of the century the total annual expenditure on the Society's Indian work did not exceed one thousand pounds. We have already commented on the absence of English candidates for its service and on its inability to vitalise the Calcutta mission.

The foundation of the Society for the Propagation of the Gospel in 1701 was an official attempt on the part of the Churches to inaugurate an aggressive and expansive policy. The participation of the state was inoffensively suggested by the grant of a royal charter, but secular patronage seems to have been confined to this. Boyle, who was a prime mover in the establishment, was a Director of the East India Company ; he seems to have been quite content to allow its sphere of activity to be restricted to the colonies and plantations of America, which by a stately but inexpensive gesture were included in the London diocese. Prince George's chaplain, before approaching the S.P.C.K., tried in vain to arouse the Society's interest in India. It failed to induce Walpole to view with active sympathy Bishop Berkeley's scheme for the revival of spiritual life in his Bermuda settlement. And its work for Georgia, from what John Wesley tells us about it, was not dramatically effective. The annual income of £800 at the close of the century represents fairly the achievements of the Church militant up to that time.

CHRISTIANITY AND GOVERNMENT OF INDIA

An age of apologetics cannot be an age of vigorous attack. Up till the time when the seed sown by Wesley and Whitefield was beginning to sprout the most Christian persons in the Church had, like William Law, withdrawn from an intractable world or, like Bishop Butler, engaged themselves in proving that Christianity was reasonable. To such apologists all enthusiasm was embarrassing. 'Pretending to be inspired by the Holy Ghost', said Butler of Whitefield, 'is a horrid thing, a very horrid thing'. Dr. Johnson, that staunch Churchman, had very similar views, and can have had little sympathy with the six undergraduates who were expelled from Oxford in 1768 for their enthusiastic talk about drawing nearer to God and inspiration. It is unjust and unwise to deal hardly with the rosy cheeked sons of the Church, or 'the cassocked huntsman' who decorated so many country parishes. They played their part in English village life. But it is impossible to imagine them as interested in the souls of our Indian subjects, and Parson Adams must have devoted more time to his classics than to S.P.C.K. reports. Watts had already produced the first missionary hymn, but it cannot often have been sung, and we hear of no more till Heber's time. With the close of the century came the fruits of the Wesleys and Whitefield. Emotionalism revived and salvation of the individual soul became more important than the stability of society. The movement with its humanitarian accompaniment gradually permeated a large section of the established church. Clapham and Cambridge began to be uneasy about India. Simeon consigned the finest of his followers to the ecclesiastical service of the Company, and they handed on the torch to Grant and Chambers during the years that the Baptist, William Carey, after his cobbler's task was done, was brooding over his map of heathen lands.

PUBLIC OPINION IN CHURCH AND STATE

The darkness that had been made visible by the pusillanimous rejection of the mission call by the Scotch Kirk Assembly in 1796, and by the Baptist President's snub to Carey in 1786, was beginning to be touched by rosy fingered dawn before the next century was well on its course. But of the established church and dissent during the eighteenth century as a whole it may fairly be said that they did little, almost nothing, to quicken a natural sense of evangelical obligations. The East India Company in its general attitude to religion in India reflected the spirit of the age in England. And that age, though it owed much to a Church which has been by some too rashly condemned, had certainly not learned from the Church what its founders had impressed on its first followers. It is doubtful whether it remembered that the Gospel meant good news. It is certain that it had no burning desire to hand it on to India. 'And this glad tidings of the kingdom shall be preached throughout the world for a witness unto all nations, and then shall the end come '.[1] It was as far back as 1560 that a reformed Church had incorporated this proclamation in its confessions. A national parliament had accepted it. But the end was not yet at hand.

[1] Confession of Faith compiled by John Knox and accepted by Scottish Parliament at Edinburgh.

PART TWO

1793–1813

PART II—1793–1813

CHAPTER IV

CAREY AND SERHAMPORE AND THE GOVERNMENT OF BENGAL

Sydney Smith and Baptist missionaries—Carey's courage and significance—his character and training—his colleague Thomas—a voyage to India—six years as an interloper in Bengal—the Baptist refugees at Serhampore—Danish hospitality and protection—progress of Serhampore settlement—Wellesley's patronage—Carey as government professor and translator—a prophet of social reform—press and other activities—Vellore Mutiny and a set-back—censure by the Government and attempted suppression—intervention of Directors—a compromise.

'If a tinker is a devout man he infallibly sets out for the East '.[1] Sydney Smith's language in moments of excitement was always incisive but occasionally incorrect. The infallibility of men such as Carey is more obvious to us than it ever can have been to him. Carey had in fact been a cobbler. But 'tinker' summarised more effectively the feelings inspired by dissenting mechanics who ventured to assume the duties entrusted by God to middle and upper class clergymen of the established church. That such men had inevitably been drawn eastwards was a generalisation characteristic of an Anglican divine of that period in a temper. It appealed to readers of the *Edinburgh Review*. But if the devout 'tinker' of Bedford had been able to rouse the eighteenth-century church even Sydney Smith himself might have experienced the eastward pull. William Carey, at all events, sailing in the Danish East Indiaman with ex-Surgeon Thomas in 1793, was the first of the 'dangerous

[1] *Edinburgh Review*, April, 1808.

band of maniacs ' who, during the next twenty years made ' insidious attempts at the conversion of India '. In his scornful rejection of men ' so totally unfitted for so important a work ', the angry Canon has much in common with the critics of the ' carpenter's Son ', in Nazareth. It was hard in Regency times not to be a snob. Even Wilberforce would have preferred a member of his class. It was morally sublime, but politically and socially embarrassing, that ' a poor cobbler working in his stall should conceive the idea of converting the Hindus to Christianity '.[1]

With William Carey begins a new era in the relations of Christian missions to the Indian Government. To the ecclesiastical student the entry of dissent on the field is interesting. We are more concerned with his boldness and determination in the face of the Company's attitude at the moment of his sailing. He was smuggled out of England and into India at a time when the Company's agents resented most bitterly the intrusion on their preserves of any unlicensed European. He belonged to a class to which a general license had most emphatically been refused. Destitute of influence and means he had found the doors of Leadenhall Street slammed in his face. With a sickly wife and a scatter-brained enthusiast he was setting out to face certain, though unknown, dangers in a land most pitiless to all who were not under the direct protection of the Company.

Carey, as we shall find later, was not solely responsible for the parliamentary change of front which led to the acceptance in 1813 of much that had been rejected in 1793. But his devotion and resolute courage played a very important part. Schwartz and Gericke had shown already that missionaries could be ' useful '. Carey was also to demonstrate the adaptability of evangelical

[1] Wilberforce's eulogy of Carey. (Coupland, *Wilberforce*.)

zeal to secular purposes. But this alone would not have secured for mission work the toleration which was ultimately guaranteed in 1813. It was Carey's obvious determination to carry out his Master's command, whether the Company willed it or no, that first convinced the parliamentary committee that they were faced by spiritual forces which it would be wiser to recognise and control than to combat. For the first time since the Reformation the conscience of the Christian world became active and real, in the evangelical field, through the speech and action of Carey. The forces of Christendom were once again consolidated for advance.

By nature and training Carey was well suited to lead such an advance. He was no brainless ranter. Enthusiasm in him was controlled and directed by a persistent and calculating mind. For several years he had brooded over his mission map, which hung in his mind as well as in the room behind his workshop. Regarding the heathen world he had, in eight laborious years, acquired, before he set out for India, a larger and more reliable store of information than any other member of the protestant churches in Europe. He had also found time to learn Latin, Greek, and Hebrew, thereby laying the foundations of his amazing linguistic career in India. Long before he had emerged from his narrow circle of Northamptonshire congregations he had realised the imperative need for prudence and forbearance, no less than for pity and for courage, in a Gospel pioneer. There must also be an inborn understanding of the heathen races and sympathetic grasp of their culture and traditions. Such indeed were the qualities and attainments that he, and all whom he has inspired in after years, acquired by nature and developed by persistent work.

This is not the place to describe the voyage of Carey and Thomas, that strangely assorted pair, which has been so well and skilfully set before us in the excellent biographies that we are lucky to possess. Carey is a man who would make every record of him live. His diaries and reports must have delighted and amazed the Baptist circles in which they went their round. It is possible for us to enjoy with Sydney Smith the vivid picture of Brother Carey, very seasick, his mind filled with consolation, as he leans over the ship's side, in contemplating the wonderful goodness of God.[1] Those who lack the imagination of the Psalmist have been permitted throughout the ages to appreciate the humour of the sea. But we shall reject the Canon's contention that those who are capable of spiritual exhilaration in such circumstances are unfit for spiritual employment. There have been others who so placed 'cried unto the Lord in their distress' and so reached the haven where they would be. And their company is more to be desired than that of society clowns.

Without a licence Carey and Thomas, on entering the Hoogly River, were no longer acceptable passengers in the Danish ship. It was from a native boat, many miles away from the port officers of Calcutta, that they set foot on soil where technically they were outlaws. The first Hindu to greet them was a convert of Thomas's, dating from the days when, inspired by the zeal of Chaplins Brown and Buchanan, he had taken up single-handed the task of healing the soul of Bengal. Ram Basu had relapsed into idolatry 'since British Christians had withheld themselves from him'. It is probable that Thomas had laid no firm foundations. For he was by nature more fit to be the loved, though frail, physician than the master builder. Firm foundations were necessary in days when conversion meant the loss of property and heritage as well as family.

In humble but safe seclusion the two lived for some

[1] *Edinburgh Review*, April, 1808.

time in the most crowded quarter of Calcutta. A hesitating visit was paid to Chaplain Brown, who, perhaps for the only time in his Indian career, failed to live up to the teaching of his master, Simeon. Not even a cooling drink was forthcoming. It may have been the absence of a licence ; probably it was the r collection of heated argument with Thomas. He was as unsound in theology as he was in finance. Many were the shocks that Carey suffered before he learned to leave neither funds nor signature in his friend's keeping.

In Calcutta, in the jungle swamps of the Sunderbands, and in the more salubrious air of Upper Bengal, Carey applied his ready hand to many trades and occupations, while he struggled, vainly as it often seemed to his home supporters, to establish a firm hold for evangelical work. At the close of this stage we find him employed as factor on the indigo estate of a wonderfully Christian planter. Udney, commercial resident of the East India Company in that area, also had a thirst for souls, and the factor was allowed to preach undisturbed to his native employees and to those of one or two like-minded planters in the neighbourhood. From Udney came the priceless favour of a printing press. But its fruits could not yet openly be displayed. For no press at this time was allowed to work outside Calcutta. The time passed not unprofitably in acquiring such a knowledge of Bengal as no European before had possessed. But he had not come to spend his days in India in commerce, however evangelically handled. In 1800 came a welcome call to battle.

Four Baptist families had been dumped in India by a Danish ship, but this time in the Danish settlement of Serhampore. The unconcealed residence of these unlicensed enthusiasts in a town only fourteen miles from Fort William, and facing Barrackpore across the river, was too much for the impetuous will of Lord Wellesley. He was far from being a foe to Christianity. Was he not at that moment planning a college for the instruction of the Company's cadets in languages, morals, and Christian principles? But orders are orders. And Cæsar had his due as well as Christ. 'Would His Excellency, the Governor of Serhampore, see to the expulsion of these interlopers, who might, at any moment violate the territories of the British East India Company?' Politely and in the course of a leisurely correspondence, but very emphatically, His Danish Excellency informed Lord Wellesley that he would do nothing of the sort. Undeterred by the threat of refusal of clearance papers by the Calcutta port authorities to the erring ship's captain, the Danish Governor, mindful perhaps of old King Frederick IV, offered the Baptist families a home, protection, and full liberty under the Danish flag. It was perhaps the only rebuff from anyone but his own Directors that Wellesley suffered in India. But he had good cause to forget it, or rather to rejoice that he received it, when the time came for him to defend in 1813 the cause of Carey and his followers in the House of Lords.

To this Danish Zoar the refugees summoned their forerunners. In 1800 Carey joined them and superintended the building up of a settlement which was shortly to dominate Calcutta and Bengal and transform the whole character of mission work in India. He had been six years in British India without a licence!

Before the close of the same year came the first converts, and Brahmins too, for whom regular instruction and a Christian life could be arranged. Bitter persecution assailed them, but the Danish authorities were firm and stoutly attended the baptism in the Hoogly. It was a triumphant end to Thomas's life of feverish failure. Joy over the first sinner brought safely home to a genuine fold is said to have hastened his collapse. The next year witnessed the complete translation of the Bible into Bengali. It was loyally sent home to George III at Windsor. 'This', said his nervous advisers, 'must come to the royal presence through the Court of Directors'. Whether it would thus have reached its destination we need not enquire. It was the royal opinion that this was beyond the Directors' jurisdiction. And the royal pleasure was expressed 'that any of my subjects should be employed (even on foreign soil) in this manner'.

The time was now at hand for a more signal proof of the confidence and esteem of those in high places. The 'base-born mechanic', ex-cobbler, ex-stowaway, ex-manager of an Indian estate, was to become collaborator with the Marquess of Wellesley in the moral and material advancement of India, by the instruction of its future rulers in piety and sound learning. There will be more to say later of the College of Fort William and its significance in the spiritual history of British Government. It is enough here to record the appointment of Carey to its staff as professor of Bengali and Sanskrit; to which was added later the chair of Marathi. Claudius Buchanan, Company's chaplain, was provost of the College; with him and his colleague Brown all details of the scheme had been elaborated. It was they who had ventured boldly to suggest the name of the leader of the settlement which had survived the imperious demand of Wellesley for its dissolution. No more graceful system of reconciliation could have been conceived by the ornaments of the established and dissenting churches than the offer and acceptance of the post. Thomas would have rejoiced to learn that Ram Basu, his first convert gathered in once more to the fold, was appointed to work as pandit under the reverend professor.

The appointment came just in time to tide the Serhampore community over what would have otherwise been an awkward period. The changes and chances of the Napoleonic wars brought Serhampore for a year under English control. But the eviction which would inevitably have followed this transfer a year before was clearly impossible when it would have entailed the loss to Government of a valued professor. His delegation to enquire into the horrors of the dedication of Hindu children to the Ganges at Saugor marks a strengthening of the links of service that bound him to the Government. His report led to the order which suppressed the practice with Welleslian abruptness. With a fresh outburst of hope he trained his students to declaim in Bengali before the possibly sceptical Governor-General on the theme that 'Asiatics are as capable of as high a civilisation as any nation of the West'. But a further report from him on the evils of suttee was for the time being fruitless. It was not till the moral support of a Hindu reformer had been secured that a Governor-General was found bold enough to follow the example of Albuquerque. Carey's report revealed the recent annihilation of 438 widows within 12 miles of Calcutta.

His activity was amazing and multifarious. Four books of the Aeneid were translated into Bengali during moments that were not claimed by Church or State. But culture and utility were rarely divorced from one another in his life. As literary adviser and translator to Government, as grammarian and lexicographer, as joint keeper of the horticultural gardens, for he was a keen and scientific gardener, and as member of the newly founded Royal Asiatic Society, he proved that he was not only indefatigable but indispensable. His oriental lore, and the wide scope of his interest, enabled him in his more distinctively evangelical undertakings 'to abstain from whatever deepens India's prejudice against the Gospel'; he never found it hard to regard the people of his adoption, not only in the mass, but individually, as his friends. And their response was eager.

Not that there was any rapid increase in the number

of his flock. The scanty tale was soon to excite the derision of his foes at home. For the personal affection inspired by Carey did not protect his converts from the most bitter forms of persecution. Every form of social service was refused. Not even the barber would approach them, as Major Scott-Waring reported with triumphant scorn.[1] Flogging and kidnapping were frequent and murder not unknown. That Indian Christians were entitled to the same protection as other members of society was not yet openly proclaimed by the authorities; individual officials were not found wanting here and there in their recognition of common justice.

But secretly the leaven was working. Most important of all perhaps was the influence brought to bear by the persistent and scholarly professor of Bengali on the young cadets of the Company who sat under him in Fort William. In our next period we shall come across several who learned from Carey that a zealous and impartial Company servant can still be and show himself by word and action a Christian. Metcalfe House in Delhi to-day reminds the official world of one of the most stalwart of Carey's students. And in the face of persecution and mistrust the work of Bible translation was carried forward. By 1806 the Serhampore press was engaged with seventeen languages. Unlicensed, and with no claim to official protection, the Baptist band from their Serhampore haven penetrated the streets of Calcutta and its surrounding villages. Their position was far less secure than that of Paul, as a Roman citizen, under the sure and constant protection of the imperial officials.

The precarious nature of their hold on Bengal was shortly to be made manifest and their boldness put to frequent and searching tests. Wellesley left India.

[1] Supporter and agent of Warren Hastings. Protagonist against missions. See p. 91.

Like his fellow Etonian, Simeon, in Cambridge, he had given to his country and its dominions unsparingly the finest qualities that the greatest school of that age could produce. There came Governors-General who 'knew not Joseph'. Carey's usefulness was often forgotten in the agitation that followed the Vellore mutiny of 1806. The effect of that incident on mission work generally will be shown later. To the Baptist cause it meant peremptory orders from Sir George Barlow for the expulsion from Serhampore of two more missionaries who had been landed there unlicensed by a Danish East Indiaman. The orders were ignored like their predecessors, but the two latest comers were expressly debarred from entering British territory. In spite of Chaplain Martyn's representation, and an admission dragged from Government that there had been no complaints received against the mission, all public preaching in British soil without express licence from the Court of Directors was stopped. Native converts might preach provided they disclaimed all connection with the mission. These terms were for the time accepted by Carey to avoid the explicit and final suppression of all evangelical work. His Indian converts at all events were boldly proclaiming their faith in the bazaars of Calcutta.

Worse trouble was to follow. Lord Minto, who replaced Barlow in 1807, was no less apprehensive. When a mission tract was brought to his notice in which Mohammed was called an impostor he had indeed just cause for complaint. As recent events in India have testified, no Government that cares for the preservation of order can afford to overlook such a public insult to Islam. It was of course a slip of which Carey would have been incapable. But it was useless for him to explain that the sentence had been inserted without his knowledge by a Moslem convert. The tract was withdrawn with apologies, but orders were issued for transfer of the mission press from Serhampore to the controlled area of Calcutta, for discontinuance of all preaching except by the Company's chaplains, and for the discontinuance of all attempts at conversion, even in private houses lent for the purpose.

This, as has been pointed out by Carey's latest biographer, is historically interesting as the first definite attempt made by a Christian Government to prohibit propagation. It was of course more than a hundred years since the East India Company had publicly connected itself with Christian enterprise ; its most friendly actions towards Christian missions had been performed, if not in secret, with a careful absence of publicity or official commitment. At the same time it is noteworthy that these very conspicuous anti-propaganda methods of Lord Minto were adopted not more than nine years after the Director's instructions that 'nothing was to be gained by disregard of the external observances of religion nor by any assimilation to eastern manners or opinion', and at a time when the Director's memorial to Schwartz was being placed finally in Madras church. Fifty years were yet to elapse before the Government of India courageously proclaimed to the Indian world 'its firm reliance on the truths of Christianity', which had never in actual fact ceased to animate its policy. It required a woman's insight to discern that a bold and open profession of a religious faith would win, rather than alienate, public confidence in India.

Meanwhile Lord Minto, though he cancelled the order for the transfer of the press, retained a tight control over its publications and resolutely forbade for several years all preaching in British territory. 'Don't you think it wrong, Dr. Carey', he asked in a 'friendly' interview, 'to try and make Indians Christians ?' It was largely due to the persistence and tact of his visitor that Lord Minto four years later, with an inconsistency that did him credit, assisted openly in the inauguration of a mission station in Agra.

Carey by this time, after the wife who had so bravely accompanied him had found release from a life of woeful perplexity, had married a relation of the Danish Governor, his own brother being at that time a night watchman at the West India Docks. But Danish influence ceased with the cession of Serhampore to the English in 1808. A band of American missionaries who arrived hopefully but unlicensed in 1811 was ignominiously expelled. Three Baptist invaders who arrived in the same year were characteristically allowed, after excursions and alarms, to stay, because, being skilled in printing affairs, they were found useful by the Government press in the cutting of Chinese type to assist the trade with China, which alone at this time remained a source of profit.

Such was the situation when the fateful year 1813 arrived in which the long-suffering Company, at the renewal of its charter, was to be deprived of the right of guarding its shores against insidious evangelists. Carey had survived twenty years of unlicensed evangelical work; the number of his colleagues and their converts had grown. The settlers as a body had made it clear that they had come to stay. They were ready and able to be useful. They consented to restrictions. But it seemed likely that their zeal would outlive the restrictions; and it was quite certain that nothing short of violence would remove them from India.

CHAPTER V

SIGNS OF GRACE. THE COMPANY AND TRUSTEESHIP

The change in last quarter of the eighteenth century—Pitt's East India Act and Trusteeship—Teignmouth, Cornwallis and Wellesley—significance of Fort William College—mission co-operation—the Company's chaplains—Henry Martyn.

THE partial suppression of Christian propaganda in Bengal, on which it has been necessary to focus attention, must not blind us to other aspects of the Company's relations to such work between 1793 and 1813. In Bengal itself up to 1806 there was much, apart from its ready use of Carey for linguistic purposes, that signified greater friendliness. Outside Bengal, and particularly in Madras, there was no definite attempt at suppression, and not a little direct encouragement; though here too the events of 1806 were prejudicial to mission work. Speaking generally we may say that British India has always produced Colonel Newcomes as well as Jos. Sedleys. Though the latter predominated up to 1793 the former is more characteristic of the period under review. The story of the Thackeray family that gave so much and owed so much to India is rich ih persons who exemplified the most lovable and least frail of the Colonel's qualities. In acts of Christian charity, as well as in the field of science, philology, and administration, it was an age of great men in India. Lord Teignmouth (Sir John Shore), despite his Clapham connection, did little as Governor-General for the moral or political prestige of the British in India. A man of simple and genuine piety, but timid and diffident, he saw no opening for the moral advancement of India except through the exercise of the Christian virtues by all servants of the Company. Though he abstained personally from official work on Sunday he shrank from ordering any closure of offices on that day. With Cornwallis and Wellesley we reach a more militant type of applied Christianity. The former by his Bengal Regulations established beyond a doubt the application of western methods and morals to eastern territories. For the privileges of conquerors was substituted a general recognition of rights and duties. When the chief secretary in his draft regulations noted, as the primary object of administration, security and advancement of the Company's interests, he was reminded that the welfare of the Company's subjects was also a primary object.

Wellesley elaborated these ethics of administration and gave them a religious basis. He was the first Governor-General who made a point of regular and official church attendance. In 1800 he attended a Nile thanksgiving service and was no doubt supported through a long sermon of Chaplain Buchanan by the force and soundness of his arguments against the revolutionary and enthusiastic tendencies of France. It was broadcast among the official community with orders against Sunday racing; and Teignmouth's orders for the church attendance of the King's regiments emerged from the oblivion to which they had been consigned. More drastic methods followed. Though there had been marked improvement in the habits and morals of the civil servants, though liberal increase in salaries had reduced speculation and removed necessity for private trade, thereby bringing to light 'only such qualities as conciliate and deserve respect', it was still clear that the temptations awaiting the cadets shipped out to India at sixteen years of age, and their ignorance of the country's ways and languages, constituted a terrible danger. Mindful of his beloved school, and with the instinct of its founder, Wellesley, in the teeth of fierce opposition (even Director Grant, disgusted by the dictator's free trade propositions, opposed him), founded and maintained the College of Fort William. Here, as the statutes remind us, 'the civil servants of the Company, no longer "the agents of a commercial concern" but guardians of "a sacred trust", were to study the people and its languages, improve their morals and fortify their minds' (by science and the classics). Here they would be 'guarded against temptation and corruption with which the nature of the climate and the peculiar depravity of the people of India will assail them'. Then and then only will they learn 'to diffuse affluence, happiness, willing obedience, and grateful attachment over every district'. And the better to insure this desirable end Chaplains Buchanan and Brown were to serve respectively as provost and vice-provost. Connection with the Church of England was vigorously to be sustained. 'Regular attendance at Divine Service will be expected from students, not as an enforced duty, but as a fit testimony in public of that proper sense of religion with which the mind of every man ought always to be impressed.' Lest this distinction should seem over subtle to cadets of 16, it was added grimly, 'Inattention to this rule will furnish the inevitable inference that the student is indifferent to the example he will have to hold forth in public employment. *Such a judgment will operate materially to the disadvantage of the student.*' Could any preacher in search of a congregation throw his net more deftly?

The pleasure that was no doubt inspired in senior members of the service by the expectation that their successors were to be fashioned as polished corners of the temple was tempered by the announcement that part of the cost was to be met by 'small contributions from the pay of all members, to be deducted annually'. But it is certain that the scheme of this μεγαλόψυχος was not merely symptomatic of a change that was coming over the whole administration, but also the cause of further change which was to bear full fruit in the days of Thomason, Edwardes, and the Lawrences. What Carey's appointment to the college signified we have already had reason to note. Further proof was forthcoming in 1812 when an ex-pupil of Carey sent from his outpost in the Moluccas a request for a batch of Serhampore missionaries. The Government, never averse from the illumination of areas outside the danger zone, responded promptly to a demand that showed a clear appreciation of what Serhampore stood for in the pioneer work of empire.

Even more characteristic of the Government's chronic fits of indifference to dangers, that at other times engrossed its meticulous attention, was the use made of the College staff and College press for various translations of the Bible and their publications. The annual list of works for which the college held itself responsible contained many entries that show how closely the college and Serhampore staff and press collaborated. Before long Baptists and Church of England chaplains were united, through their associations on the staff, in forwarding the undenominational work of the Bible Society, which had been established in Calcutta under the auspices of several judges and members of the council ; towards the translation of the Bible into Malay a grant was explicitly sanctioned by the Government.

Simultaneously in south India the work of the S.P.C.K. Danish missionaries was allowed to expand. They were permitted to accept a pressing invitation from Travancore. To the admission of representatives of the recently established London Mission no objection was raised.

Mission work in Bombay began with the despatch of a Serhampore missionary thither at the request of the Advocate-General Mackintosh. The same Presidency in 1812 offered a shelter to the American missionaries expelled from Bengal after a year's odyssey in the Indian ocean.

The bold persistence of the Company's chaplains during this period in reminding the authorities of Christian obligations deserves recognition. Buchanan, Brown, Thomason,[1] Corrie[2] and Martyn were men of a very different stamp from the time-serving men, only too ready to add to their official emoluments, who had been so often forgetful of their duties in the eighteenth century. Inspired by John Newton and Simeon they were far from ashamed to confess the faith. Some of them, particularly Henry Martyn, devoted themselves openly to the task of conversion, so far as it was compatible with their establishment duties, and met all criticism by a reminder that under the Charter Act of 1698 they were not only allowed but ordered 'to instruct the Gentoos'. Martyn seems to have devoted much of his time to the Mohammedan portion of the population and to Arabic and Hindustani translations of the Bible.

The story of Henry Martyn's all too brief crusade has been admirably told but a short time ago. His years in India were too few to permit of his doing much in person, for the christianisation of the government, but the general effect of his life on public opinion at home and in India was incalculable. He had been the first candidate for Church Missionary Society work in 1802; though circumstances prevented his inclusion in their ranks he was, through the fiery zeal of his spirit, largely responsible for the rapid advance which that society was soon to make. At Cawnpore and Dinapore

[1] Father of the well-known civil servant. See p. 123.

[2] Subsequently Bishop of Madras.

he and Corrie were known as 'the black Chaplains' and endured in consequence for some time a social boycott. But socially the vitality and abundance of his friend and disciple, Mrs. Sherwood, must have compensated him. That resolute lady, wife of the paymaster of the 85th Foot, was at the time half-way in a triumphant progress from 'Susan Gray', historically the first effort to 'inculcate Christian principles in the poor', to her story of the Fairchild family. Though she had not yet begun the first of her four volumes of talks on confirmation to young females of upper and middle-class ranks, she was already meditating that matchless account of 'little Henry and his Bearer' which was for so many years to support the cause of mission work and spread an effective, though limited, knowledge of Indian life in English mid-Victorian homes. Henry Martyn needed no human inspiration. But his frail body owed much to her ministrations, which enabled him to emulate her energy; the best Arabic scholar of his day in India, and largely responsible for the standardisation of Urdu, he proved pre-eminently what it was the glory of so many Christian workers to manifest in the first half of the last century, that neither evangelical zeal nor administrative duties need prevent an evangelist from studying the literature and customs of the peoples he wishes to serve.

Faced by zeal such as Martyn's it was useless for an indignant commandant of artillery at Benares to protest against his men being compelled to attend divine service at such a distance from the lines, or for Lord Moira to complain that Thomason's rebuke for a breach of Sunday observance was hardly such as a Governor-General of India should be expected to receive. In, and as the Company sometimes thought, out of season the gallant band did not cease to urge on the good work, here by quiet influence in Fort William College and there by pressing on all the claims of the Bible Society ; now by getting government help for Bible translation, and again by excogitation of schemes for comprehensive mission enterprise, or for enhancing the dignity and prestige of the Church in India by an episcopal establishment. What Buchanan accomplished in England outside his Indian work will separately be shown.

CHAPTER VI

THE VELLORE MUTINY AND REACTION

The Vellore outbreak—origin and effect on missions—Directors' indecision—absence of historical grounds for apprehension—Hindu ideas of Church and State—Indian attitude towards previous rulers of alien faith—misunderstanding due to lack of policy, firmness and information.

MUCH of the seed sown with such tact and zeal by the Baptists of Serhampore and the Company's chaplains during these years was rendered ineffective by the events of 1806. To us who know how the British Government weathered the storm of 1857, and emerged more resolute than ever to advance the moral progress of India, the commotion caused by the mutiny of the Company's troop at Vellore, and the moral and spiritual cowardice that ensued, is difficult to understand. But there were other contributory causes. The actual occasion of the mutiny was a possibly tactless order regarding the sepoy's head-dress. Advantage was taken by relatives of Tippu Sahib of Mysore, resident in the neighbourhood, and still smarting under a sense of humiliation and exile. It is more than probable that they worked skilfully on the fanaticism of the sepoys and that tales of an intensive religious campaign by their masters were afloat. But the Commander-in-Chief at Madras was convinced that no action by Government in support of mission work, and no indiscretion on the part of any mission, had been directly or indirectly responsible for the outbreak.

The Mutiny none the less brought a recrudescence of the timidity that had periodically paralysed the

Company; its after effects were felt for many years after Parliament in 1813 threw open its territories to missionaries. For many years it weakened all efforts for the social and moral amelioration of India. This is the more surprising as the list of fanatical outbreaks under British rule in India up to 1806 was neither long nor awe-inspiring. There had been of course the Sanyasi uprising in Bengal in 1771, and there had been some troublesome disturbance among the Maravars of Tinnevelly in 1805. It is difficult to believe that the general record was such as to necessitate or justify the Bengal campaign against the Serhampore Mission which has been described above, or the subsequent expulsion from Madras of the London Mission agents who had been admitted only a few years before. But there was everywhere the uneasiness of men who resented the intrusion of firebrands into a powder magazine. This in fact was the metaphor employed by Lord Hastings in deprecating seven years later the expansion of mission work northwards.

So rumours began to circulate at official dinners, and minutes were prepared in which all incidents and tendencies that could possibly be misconstrued by native opinion as signs of Government's desire for proselytes were laboriously collected. The grants to Schwartz and others, the interest shown by individual officials in the Bible Society's work, the schemes by government chaplains, supported by men who were now Directors, for bishops and comprehensive mission campaigns, and more particularly the Bible translation work that was being so jealously pushed forward by missionaries in government employ with the help of government press and pandits! All this seemed to nervous minds calculated inevitably to excite suspicion and hatred. Apparently ignorant of India's past, refusing to recognise the fact that India expected of her rulers a firm profession of their faith, and had never resented open patronage of the religion professed by her previous alien rulers, they resumed a course of compromise and evasion, occasional patronage followed by apparent suppression, which ultimately inspired the Indian world with vague and very real mistrust and was among the causes of the Indian Mutiny.

The Directors at home were sorely puzzled. Yielding to the influence of Charles Grant and Shore they had in 1798 urged their servants in no uncertain terms to remember that it was not only possible but ultimately politic for the rulers of India to profess and call themselves Christians. But these instructions gave place after the events of 1806 to shifting and vacillating expressions of opinion. What in fact could the poor men do, with the Board of Control watching every movement, Wilberforce on their doorstep, Grant in their council chamber, and the shareholders clamouring for security and dividends ?

Their despatches commenting on the Minto Serhampore controversies of 1807–8 create an impression of the Almighty slightly worsted in his negotiations with Mammon. It must be admitted that so far no damage had been done by enthusiasm. Dr. Carey seemed a very prudent gentleman. The peaceful and unobtrusive circulation of Bibles and pamphlets need not necessarily cause a breach of the peace. On the other hand nothing could have been wiser than the suppression of public preaching. Perhaps the Government might see its way to the permission of preaching in private chapels and mission houses. Could the native converts be expected to understand the English services of the Company's chaplains which apparently were to be their spiritual pasture ? The Government is of course responsible for order and security. You have done well to control mission publications. Doubtless Dr. Carey will recognise the need and advantages of such control.

Do not let it be supposed for one moment, so the tortuous excuse for the uncertain seat on the fence continued, that we deprecate the diffusion of Christianity in India. But we do deprecate imprudence ; not that we assert there has been such imprudence. In particular we discourage all unnecessary and ostentatious interference by Company servants with religious prejudice. At the same time (seeing that so many of our Directors support the Bible Society) we find it hard to condemn their interest in evangelical work. But will Mr. Chaplain Claudius Buchanan remember that he must not forward mission memorials to a perplexed Governor-General with an immoderate endorsement ? and could the Governor-General understand that, though zeal requires a check, it is better to deal with missionaries (who are not zealots) by interviews and homely talk than through official resolutions ? and finally that naughty suggestion by the Government that there was no need for any increase in the number of missionaries was most indiscreet. Was it not realised in India that many of the 'Meritorious' propagandists were not missionaries, and that all missionaries since 1793 had proceeded to India without waiting to ask the poor slighted Directors for a licence ?

It was high time indeed that Parliament should take the matter out of the hands of such poor spirited evaders of the point. India calls for a firm purpose and a clear and confident expression of it. Fortunately there were men at work in England who had learned at last how to set the parliamentary machine in motion. But before passing from the Company to those who are preparing to take from them a decision which was beyond its powers, it is worth while briefly to emphasize the absence of historical support for their vacillation.

The Hindu idea of kingship, as revealed in their history, includes the determination and patronage of a state religion. Toleration of other religions was usually expected and vouchsafed. But in any case a ruler who did not openly proclaim his gods and see to their proper worship and maintenance was not the king the Hindu world expected. It is difficult to believe that there would have been any serious disturbance in the most orthodox Hindu circles if the British Government from the start had adopted the bold and frank policy which Asoka's pillars record in widely separated parts of his empire. Adopting definitely the view that the ruler is responsible for the welfare of his subjects, he commends to their attention the Buddhist precepts as a necessary corrective of the Brahminical predominance. 'In the happiness of his subjects lies his happiness, in their welfare his welfare'; his words seem often to anticipate the Queen's proclamation of 1858. And to secure their happiness he tells them of the way, as Queen Victoria was to refer later, to the faith on which she relied so firmly. To teach the way, or Dharma, he would arrange for periodical tours by his officials who would train them in self-control, reverence for all men, even slaves, and humanity. Under the gentle influence of education, animal sacrifice should be abandoned, wells dug, trees planted, and hospitals built in all parts of his dominions. In token of his passionate belief he was sending out his missionaries into all lands.

What his emissaries did for Ceylon may be seen to-day in the buildings and life of that island. The later results of the activity he inspired may be seen in Burma and more distant lands. Though Buddhism as a separate religion soon faded in India, Asoka left his permanent mark on Indian life and thought. But for our purpose what signifies is the fact that this clear statement of the ruler's faith and aims was accompanied by no violence and no pressure; it aroused, so far as we know, among his subjects no outbreak of fanatical opposition.

The Hindu has always respected in others the clear

signs of an alien faith and evidence of a sincere and disinterested desire for his own spiritual advancement. Having no definite and crucial doctrines exposed to attack, he is of all races the most tolerant of other men's dogmas. Within his own continent he has seen Brahminism gradually but persistently extended by peaceful penetration and by the absorption of animistic races. Himself averse from religious persecution, he has been accustomed generally to expect from alien rulers a similar extension. It cannot be said that his previous history, taken as a whole up to 1800, had made him nervous and suspicious of the intentions of such aliens.

The Portuguese, it is true, had employed religious pressure in their territories, but they had been wise enough to exclude from all risk of suppression or exacerbation the higher caste Hindus who were commercially, and in administration, so useful to them. Their policy of preference for Christians seems to have roused little resentment. The attitude of their Mohammedan conquerors had been similar. There had of course in early days been fanatics whose ruthless propagation of Islam invariably defeated its own purpose. But from a fairly early date, and throughout most of the Mogul period, the Mohammedan rulers were far from fanatical. The Moguls had been wise enough to appreciate the indispensability of their Hindu employees, and to avoid any measures likely to alienate or annoy them; their Hindu wives had helped them to understand the Hindu attitude. The mysticism and comparative geniality which tinged their religious outlook, as a result of their contact with Persia, restrained them from forcible conversion or destruction of temples, or any frontal attack on caste. Only the bigoted Aurungzeb attempted such measures, which, it is true, were largely responsible for the downfall of the Mogul Empire. It is not of course suggested that his method, or even those of the Portuguese, could have been adopted with impunity by the British. But a race that had endured for so long without serious outbreaks alien rulers who openly professed a fundamentally different faith, and who were not above applying gentle pressure by preferential treatment of fellow-worshippers and the imposition of a special tax on infidels, was not likely to be goaded into revolt by rulers who proclaimed abroad their Christianity, and tolerated and protected its evangelists. But how would they view the assault made on caste by a religion which must necessarily show open antagonism to that sacred institution? This was the question that harassed the apprehensive rulers of India throughout the early years of the nineteenth century. The social persecution and the sometimes murderous assaults directed against native converts seemed to supply a convincing answer. But if they had probed the Hindu mind more deeply they would have been reassured.

It was natural that Hindu orthodoxy should defend itself by such methods, for it was clever enough to see that under a Government that shrank from protection of its rivals aggression was the best mode of defence. There is nothing in the previous history of India that suggests a similar attitude towards the millions of conversions to Islam that had been effected, and were still being effected under British rule. Few if any of their Mohammedan rulers would have tolerated for one moment such an attitude, nor did the impracticability of such measures lead to any violent explosion of repressed feeling. The British in India have always been inclined to over-estimate Hindu susceptibility in the matter of caste. They have not realised that most of the great Hindu reformers, and they had been many in number since the Buddha's time, have openly and with impunity declaimed against the dangers and perversion of that institution. Some of the greatest and most popular Hindu poets brought all their art to bear upon it. Kabir and Tukaram are not the less familiar and loved in Hindu households because many of their most gifted verses proclaim invincibly the brotherhood of men. To the Hindu a holy man remains holy whatever his views on caste. And as such he is entitled to royal protection. No trouble would have been excited by a Government that protected unflinchingly the Christians, so long as their campaign was inspired by love and directed by tactful sympathy. Such campaigns the present writer has often found in being, unimpeded and unsuspected, in the very citadels of Hindu orthodoxy. What the Hindu failed to understand and watched with ever-growing suspicion was a Government that oscillated between covert acceptance, or even carefully veiled approval, of evangelists, who were spreading what was presumably their own religion, and nervous disavowal of them and all their work. And when in later years this same intriguing Government opened and supported schools which, without open profession of religion, undermined the very foundations of caste, it is small wonder that they attributed to such mysterious rulers the most sinister designs on their institutions. The Indian Mutiny was the outcome, not of any fear or dislike of Christianity, but of genuine misunderstanding of a Government which had failed to take India into its confidence or to announce how far it was definitely prepared to go in the protection of those who were trying morally and spiritually to heal her. There was no perfect love that casteth out fear, no glorious liberty that is the birthright of the sons of God.

The attitude of Islam has always been different and more difficult. But Islam in India since the sixteenth century has never been the same as Islam in Arabia or Egypt. The more genial attitude of the semi-Persian

Moguls influenced their Moslem subjects. The evolution of that composite language, Urdu,[1] the adoption of purda by the Hindus, and of saint worship by the Moslem, symbolised and assisted a growing tolerance. It was not of course proof against acts of bigotry on either side. A word against the moral character or motives of the Prophet, or the parade of idols before a mosque, on the one side, and an obviously offensive exhibition of cow-killing on the other, has always been enough to produce streams of blood. But a Government bold enough to stop resolutely any such offensiveness, if indeed such a check has ever been required by the work of Christian missions in India, and determined on the other hand to secure a fair field for any tactful exposition of doctrines however antagonistic to Islam, has never excited dangerous animosity in Islamic India. Those who with extreme orthodoxy have protested against the exercise of temporal power by infidels have always been in a very distinct and submerged minority. The occasional emergence of such orthodoxy, as for instance with the Ali brothers[2] in 1920, has been for the most part a political device calculated to embarrass the authorities rather than to appease the conscience. In fact, the Moslem like the Hindu in India has always been reluctant to oppose authority that boldly proclaims its determination to insist on a fair field without favour.

[1] Camp language of the Mogul armies ; a blend of Hindi and Persian.

[2] Mohammad and Shauquat Ali ; leaders of the Khilaphat (pro-Turkish) party in India in 1920.

CHAPTER VII

FINAL TRIUMPH OF WILBERFORCE

Wilberforce and Clapham at work again—their opponents—Champions of Hinduism—and 'defeatists'—the 'inconvertible Hindu'—their supporters—Southey and the *Quarterly Review*—foundation and significance of C.M.S. and Bible Society—growing mistrust of the Company—Parliamentary Committee and its witnesses—debate in Lords and Commons—Wellesley's tribute to missions—the open door secured—and ecclesiastical establishment—and acknowledgments of educational responsibility.

We must now return for a while to England. Moving in and out among the vacillating Directors, and watching their tortuous course with shrewd humorous eyes and a persistent purpose, William Wilberforce, with all the disappointment of his 1793 defeat set resolutely behind him, has been at work with 'deliberate speed, majestic instancy'. He has not forgotten that the charter of the East India Company has again to be renewed by Parliament in 1813. Apart from the recurring opportunity of bringing pressure to bear on an elusive Company, there is always the Board of Control, Pitt's instrument for controlling the more important functions of the Directors' Court and insisting on the Court's policy being consistent with the will of Parliament. This Board, by the date we have now reached, consists merely of a President, a member of the Government, who is advised by the secret committee, composed of Directors nominated by the Court for this purpose. Through and with this Committee the President is kept in touch with all the Directors' doings. He can even communicate his orders direct to the

Governor-General and receive reports from him, unperturbed and unprejudiced by the rumours and intrigues of secretariats in India and of Leadenhall Street. With the Parliament he represents will rest the final decision on this missionary question which Wilberforce sees can no longer indefinitely be delayed.

The activity and manifold devices of an attractive intriguer are recorded for our admiration in the letters and diary extracts of Wilberforce. Little did the millions, committed but for him to the providential protection of Brahma, realise the speed and adroitness with which he passed from Lambeth to Leadenhall Street, from Clapham to Whitehall, in his pursuit of directors, bishops, members of Parliament, shareholders and cabinet ministers, always tactful, conciliatory, and determined. 'Great is the glory, for the strife is hard.' First among his opponents is the *Edinburgh Review* with Sydney Smith as its protagonist. It would not be fair to say that hatred of dissent was the sole or even the primary cause of the bitter hostility to missions that informs every page of the 1808 article. But the prominent part played by the 'Low and base-born mechanics', who were called Baptists or Anabaptists as best fitted the rhythm of the sentence, certainly suggested to the writer his best epithets and quips. The apprehension, masking itself under an air of righteous indignation and contempt, which these attacks betray has already been illustrated by extracts with which the atmosphere of 1793 was represented. Timely backing was given by the writings of civilian military officers returned from India, untouched apparently by the ministrations of Buchanan and Brown, or by 'the Washerwoman of Finchley Common' which even Jos. Sedley had read during a few hours' storm at sea. Perhaps like Jos. they had come across the wrong kind of missionary. But there were not many Silas Hornblowers in the India of that time. Whatever the cause, Thomas Twining ' of Calcutta and the Customs ', much interested in tea and mercantile security, Major Scott-Waring, once agent in England of Warren Hastings, and Colonel Stewart, reported vaguely as a convert to Hinduism but perhaps the first of the Theosophists, were vocally insistent in their denunciation of ' illiterate ranting fanatics, despised by respectable Hindus, engaged in converting the scum of the earth '.[1] ' Crawling from the holes and caverns of their original destinations ', said Charles Marsh, ex-barrister of Madras, ' these apostates from the loom and the anvil, these renegades from the lowest handicraft ', were endangering the security of the Empire and the peaceful innocence of happy homes.

It may have been dim recollections of a carpenter's bench in Galilee that caused so often an abrupt transition from an incomplete catalogue of dissenters' trades to an ardent recital of the dangers that they brought in their train. They must have made the flesh of many a stock-holder creep, as he read how patronage of the Bible Society made his dividends almost less than hypothetical, and how the translation of the Bible by Government employees placed the lives of those who were wishing to make them rich in imminent and unprecedented peril. Visions of Hindus dedicating bloodstained hands to Kali, and of Mohammedans panting for a Jehad, haunted their dreams.

Some of these pamphlets displayed what even the tactful Wilberforce had to stigmatise as ' a distinct partiality for Pagan religion '. It is improbable that many were genuinely attracted by the fanaticism that they had so powerfully described. Their partiality

[1] This and the following passages are quoted in the *Edinburgh Review* article of May, 1808.

implied rather a preference of paganism to dissent, and of idolatrous but wealthy merchants to puritanical cobblers. Mr. Charles Marsh was unable to conceal his surprise and horror when he saw attempts at conversion among 'a cheerful and well-ordered society, refreshed by the benign and softening influence of religion and morality, with a system of manners founded on mild and polished obedience, preserving the surface of social life smooth and unruffled'. He does not seem to have gone below the surface, or to have read the report of Dr. Carey on the 'softening influence' of the Saugor dedications and of Jonathan Duncan, the civil servant, on the 'cheerful and well-ordered' system of infanticide in Benares.

More plausible and less easy at that time to meet by statistics were the arguments of the 'defeatists'. Hindus it is well known were inconvertible. Why sacrifice the affluence of English homes and the peace of India to an idle dream? Better 'wait till the Almighty shall be pleased to lead them into the paths of light and truth'.

Before many years were out the Abbé Dubois,[1] after thirty-one years of patient work in India, was to arrive at similar conclusions. This careworn and essentially Christian-hearted Roman Catholic missionary, who had lived for and with the high-caste Hindus of South India, who had collected information about their habits and institutions that have been of the utmost value ever since to western workers for India, who had ventured to undertake tasks in the kingdom of Tippu that no other emissary of Government had ever dared, published as a final result of his labours the most pessimistic forecast

[1] Dubois worked in India, 1792–1823. For further information on his career and views see Beauchamp's edition of *Hindu manners, customs, and ceremonies*. Clarendon Press. He gave equally gloomy evidence before the Parliamentary Committee of 1832, reporting that the number of R.C. Christians was visibly declining.

that has ever emanated from a genuine Christian. In his letters on the state of Christianity in India, which were translated and published in England, he shows how, after 'watering the soil of India with his tears', the seed sown by him had 'fallen upon a naked rock and instantly died away'. 'Disgusted at the total inutility' of his pursuits he tells how two-thirds of the Jesuit converts had disappeared. During the last sixty years there had been in the higher castes practically no proselytes. In thirty years he had made three hundred converts, of whom two-thirds were pariahs. This was due not merely to converts' loss of civil rights and the infamy they incurred, not even to their hatred of the foreigner, nor to the immoral lives of Europeans, but essentially to the innate vileness of Hinduism and its centuries of sequestration from the world.

What the Catholic orders, with their discipline, the supporting majesty of the universal Church, and their studied adaptation of non-essentials, even perhaps essentials, to the carefully studied lives of the people, had failed to accomplish must surely be beyond the powers of sectarians depending only on the Bible. The Bible! 'You must erase from the code of the Christian religion the cardinal precept of charity if you are to appeal to this caste-ridden folk.' And how will the tale of the fatted calf be told to these worshippers of the cow? Can a carpenter's son, whose disciples are fishermen, speak to the hearts of Brahmins who will not eat with Sudras defiled by manual work? Let us remember rather that 'Whom he will he hardeneth'. 'If the community be not worthy let your peace return to you.' Let us shake the dust off our feet and remember that 'if you try to change a single institution you will find an ungovernable people. The day when Government shall presume to interfere in such matters will be the last of its political existence'. A few years after these words were written suttee was abolished, amid protest it is true, but there was no uprising and the Government survives. William Wilberforce did not know India as Dubois or even Thomas Twining knew it. But he knew the Bible and had a text at his command more potent than any urged by Dubois. The Hindu might be a saint, as Charles Marsh had said, or he might be a fanatic, deaf to all appeal, as Dubois and Sydney Smith declared. If he was a saint he deserved the Gospel ; if he was a caste-ridden idolator he needed it. In any case he was a man and a brother, and Wilberforce was going to show him the way to the common Father of mankind. And now there is just time before I go to dine with Charles Grant for a letter to Bishop Porteous[1] to remind him about that meeting and to Castlereagh[2] to tell him he is in charge of the Commons' Resolution, and to Wellesley to bring him up to the scratch in the House of Lords. Things are very different now from what they were in 1793.

Wilberforce himself was showing more care and tact than in those impetuous days. In the first place, much as he admired the Methodists, their open support was to be deprecated as embarrassing. 'Sorry rascals', his friend Pitt had called them, 'We will keep them in the background'. Not too much talk of Serhampore. The Church Missionary Society, which even Bishops have smiled on, though they do not seem active in its support, is a better card to play. And perhaps we were rather abrupt in suggesting the open patronage of Government. Why not push as a substitute that capital plan for an episcopal establishment in India that Buchanan has brought home with him ? Most respectable and can't be gainsaid even by Sydney Smith. We

[1] Bishop of London. Supporter of C.M.S. and Bible Society.
[2] Foreign Secretary and Leader of House of Commons, 1813.

might even get his brother Bobus[1] to move it in the House. One for the Canon that!

Bishop Porteous too has promised his support; seems ready to include India in his diocese to make up for the loss of America. Then there are the chosen vessels at Leadenhall Street. Grant is a tower of strength and Teignmouth far more daring and alive than he ever was in India. President of the Bible Society too. At Westminster we can count on Liverpool[2] and Castlereagh, Perceval[3] and Vansittart.[4] And there is that dear good Claudius Buchanan, home from India, full of wrath against Minto for objecting to his memorial on behalf of Serhampore and for having suppressed the Directors' eulogy of Schwartz. He is devoting his salary and private means to founding prizes for dissertations and poems on mission work in every part of the country. And Southey was splendid in the last *Quarterly Review*

How far Southey's spirited contribution to the *Quarterly Review* in 1809 was inspired by mere hatred of Sydney Smith who had enlivened the buff and yellow rag in 1808, and how far it was the product of genuine piety, is not for us to determine. It is good reading to-day though it may have been embarrassing to the mission party when it appeared. In asking Government to give special preference in the disposal of loaves and fishes to native converts he certainly went beyond his brief. 'Let not Government touch my work; it can only succeed in making them hypocrites; I wish to make them Christians'. Few, if any, British missionaries in India have repudiated those words of Carey. Southey is on surer ground when he counters the panic-mongers and

[1] Robert Percy Smith, elder brother of Sydney; Advocate-General of Bengal, 1803–1810.

[2] Second earl. Prime Minister in 1813.

[3] Prime Minister, 1809–1812. The resolution was moved in 1812.

[4] Chancellor of the Exchequer in 1813. Son of a Bengal civil servant.

explodes the fears of fanatical uprising. By timely references to past history he reminds his readers of what even Tippu Sahib had done without danger to his throne and how Duncan's suppression of infanticide in Benares had caused no serious trouble. His defence of the Baptists though patronising was salutary and sound. They had at any rate accomplished what all the princes and potentates of the world, and all the universities and establishments *into* the bargain, had shrunk from attempting. The plea that India's civilisation needs no Gospel is met by a denunciation of Hindu literature and philosophy which is a remarkable anticipation of Macaulay's minute a quarter of a century later.[1] Caste is not invincible nor are Hindus inconvertible. 'Only by Christianising the natives can we strengthen and secure ourselves.' The path of duty and policy is always the same. The Scotch Kirk's plea[2] that the procedure is 'preposterous', though not directly quoted, is met substantially by the words, 'The first step towards winning the natives to our religion is to show them that we have one'. A Church that would remain effective must be a proselytising Church. Let us be up and doing, remembering that 'If England were now dispossessed of Eastern Dominions the Hindu historians would urge that we had no religion . . . just as travellers do of the Hottentots!'

Such was the valiant support that was endorsed by the creation of the third great missionary society of the Church of England. How the Society for the Propagation of the Gospel had been tied by official restraint and by the fact that its charter confined its activities to British possessions in the Western world we have already seen. The Society for Promotion of Christian

[1] In favour of western education for India, 1835.
[2] 1796. See p. 28.

Knowledge, with limited funds and activities at home as well as abroad, had done its best to supplement the Indian efforts of Danes and Germans. The Church Missionary Society that arose in 1799 out of the deliberations of the Eclectic Society—on Botany Bay and allied topics—announced its aim boldly and tactfully as supplementary to that of the S.P.G. Established definitely for work in Africa and the East, it avoided all suspicion of rivalry to the older and officially recognised body. Backed only by staunch churchmen it escaped the associations that still prejudiced the work of the Baptist Society and its follower the London Missionary Society (1793). At the same time its evangelical traditions and foundations made it more attentive to individual needs, more intent on the essentially Christian sport of 'soul hunting', than was possible for a society whose official representation of the Church as a whole restrained its evangelical tendencies and regulated its pace by the misgivings of the most cautious bishops. For the society the episcopal bench, though not hostile, did nothing individually or as a body for the first fourteen years. It was the zeal of free-lances, lay as well as clerical, that brought its annual income by 1812 to the then respectable sum of £1300. Though many years were to elapse before the ordinary layman was to be able to view without humorous irritation the impetuous ardour of Mrs. Jellaby and Lady Walham,—Thackeray reminds us constantly how strong the prejudice of the first half-century was,—statesmen such as Perceval, Liverpool, and Bathurst, as well as Directors of the East India Company, were among its open supporters. Lady Kew might rave against the tyranny that shut up her grandson in a room 'with a basin of gruel and Watts' hymns'. But Sophia Alethea Newcome kept a good table and had a five-pound note as well as a copy of *Little Henry and his Bearer* ready for her step-grandson.

Clapham had learned that piety and comfort are not irreconcilable.

If the Church Missionary Society and tactful Wilberforce prevented the dissenting element from being too obtrusive in support, the British and Foreign Bible Society, founded in 1804, provided common ground on which churchmen and sectarians could combine to produce an atmosphere which was shortly to impress the parliamentary committee. Though Wilberforce had once opposed the repeal of the Test Act, and even now found dissent embarrassing, he was ready for co-operation when sectarianism was decently veiled by the enveloping respectability of Clapham. By all means therefore let Teignmouth serve as its president.

Other Directors' names were soon enrolled; with foot thus firmly inserted they could prevent an abrupt closure of the Leadenhall Street door.

The time indeed for any such abruptness had now passed. Their own vacillation and the stress of circumstances had brought the Directors to a point when it was no longer possible for them to defend effectively the privileges and dictatorial rights that they had maintained in 1793. The sands were running out. Trade for them had suffered in the Napoleonic wars and Wellesley's confoundedly insubordinate policy of 'forward' had led to a financial crisis. Imperial glory and responsibilities were all very well; but they were not compatible with steady dividends. It was no longer financially easy to secure parliamentary backing of their privileges; and those members of the Government who were not showing absurd and meticulous interest in their work as 'Trustees' were inclined to grumble when the question of a Government loan for the fit performance of a Trustee's duties was raised. Every one in short seemed to be more interested in their duties than in their rights. Even their staunch friend—in Mission affairs—the *Edinburgh Review*, was reminding its readers that 'The State of their Indian Empire has uniformly disappointed the hopes and expectations of the Company'. 'Feelings of most painful anxiety and regret' attended a spectacle of 'political and commercial embarrassment.' While 'golden prospects of national revenue' are receding, 'A Commander-in-Chief occasions a sanguinary conspiracy at Vellore—to effect a change in the dress of the sepoys.'[1]

Was it perhaps possible that the surrender of some of its dearly bought rights would be necessary in order to preserve the remainder and to stop this troublesome preoccupation with 'duties'?

Bravely none the less did the Directors prepare for a last stand when a parliamentary committee began to prepare the way for the charter renewal of 1813. The records of that committee present an entertaining picture of petitions from evangelical unions and counter petitions from mercantile associations, of heterogeneous witnesses, ex-Governors-General, missionaries, military heroes and collectors of Bogglywallah, herded together in the waiting-room. Warren Hastings, before a full committee of the House that rose to show its respect, was able to recall his meeting with Schwartz 'a very worthy gentleman' and his benevolent interest in 'a conversion by Kiernander'. 'Could he conceive a situation in which missionaries, unlicensed and without restraint, could be conducive to order?' Well, no, he wouldn't like to go so far. Really 'he could not encourage such a situation'. And so he passed out to resume his exercises in Latin verse that were so much more restful and satisfying to a tired mind, He 'dared not say all that was in his mind on the subject; it is one of great hazard'. Perhaps his old friend Scott-Waring could oblige. A most experienced and sensible man.

[1] Vol. xv, 1810.

Lord Teignmouth, with brother Directors at his back itching to pull his coat-tails, though cautious as became his character and official record, was far more reassuring than his greater predecessor. Government support of missions! Certainly not! This had always been and remained dangerous and impracticable. Nothing that the Government had ever done had produced or was likely to produce such an impression in native minds. The people of India had at last realised that it was the intention of the Government to tolerate and protect their religions. Here there must have been a cough from Wilberforce. No harm could possibly come from the inclusion by the Government of its own religion in the protected list.

The hour approached at last when the amazing versatility and persistence of Wilberforce were to meet their reward. In 1812 Castlereagh's resolution 'that it is our duty to promote the interests and happiness of the native inhabitants of the British Dominions in India and that such measures ought to be adopted as may tend to the introduction among them of useful knowledge, and of religious and moral improvement' was carried in a House of 125 by 52 votes. But a similar success in 1793 had been followed by disaster when the charter had come up for renewal. This time Wilberforce had heavier artillery and concentrated his fire; to the revived resolution had been appended a declaration in favour of 'sufficient facilities to those going to India for these benevolent designs'. When the time came for remodelling the charter accordingly, there was no longer any talk of Government patronage and maintenance. There was not even any explicit reference to missionaries as apart from other philanthropists. But the resolution was incorporated in a clause, the previous designs were made financially practicable by providing for the annual allotment by the Company of one lakh of rupees for the revival and improvement of literature and the introduction and promotion of a knowledge of the sciences ; and the tactful omission in this particular connection of a reference to religion was amply made good by the adroit settlement of the licensing question. Though here again the claims of missionaries received no separate recognition, provision was made for the reference of all cases of refusal of licences to the Board of Control. And the debate made it clear that the *onus probandi* for all licences refused to missionaries would rest with the Directors. The Board of Control, by insisting on licences for all missionaries who would in other capacities or professions have been regarded as eligible applicants, would be carrying out what was obviously the will of Parliament. The right of entry for Christian workers was in fact at last firmly established. And from a Government now definitely committed by their charter to a policy of moral advancement, as well as to financial backing of the same, not merely toleration but the protection of Christian evangelists might reasonably be expected.

Such were the results of twenty years of patient and persistent work and of experience based on disappointment. It was in vain for expert authority[1] to protest in the final stages that 'the religion of the Hindus was pure and unexceptionable' and that 'he would rather save the lives of 30,000 fellow-countrymen in India than save the souls of all Hindus at so dreadful a price'. The word of Lord Wellesley in 'another place' carried more weight. 'While I was in India I never knew of any danger arising from the missionaries' proceedings. They are a quiet, ordered, discreet and learned body. I thought it my duty to have the Scriptures translated

[1] Henry Montgomery. A retired civil servant to be distinguished from later bearer of same name on pp. 121-195.

into the tongues of the East. A Christian Governor could not do less than this. A British Governor could not do more.'

Nor did this complete the triumph of Wilberforce. In renewing the charter, Parliament did not merely open the door to missionaries and announce its sympathy with their general purpose. The time had come for a gesture that would make clear to all, with a minimum of expense and risk, that the Government, as a Government, intended to provide in a dignified manner for the more appropriate exercise of the religion that it professed. The scheme proposed ten years before by Claudius Buchanan was at last to bear fruit. The morals and religious exercises of the Company's servants and troops in India were consigned to the supervision of a bishop and three archdeacons. The chaplains, now at last legalised, and enriched by the addition of a Presbyterian colleague, were to be stimulated and directed at last by local overseers. 'Something royal in a spiritual and temporal sense'; such had been Buchanan's vision. Something for the mind to rest on and the eye to contemplate. Bishops in fact to look up to, with India watching awestruck the spiritual subjection of its temporal rulers.

This side of the proposal however must not be made too prominent. When Lord Teignmouth assured the Committee that the appearance of a bishop in India 'would be viewed with perfect indifference', any surprise that he may have occasioned in the episcopal world must have been blended with a feeling of relief that they were to be employed in no explosive schemes. Wilberforce made it sufficiently clear that he was to be in no way responsible for mission work, and that his appointment would suggest no association of Government with that work. But the provision though humble was the characteristically neat rounding off of a design that gave legal security and protection to all reasonable and prudent measures for demonstrating that England was a Christian country and wished India to be the same. Something had been gained since Lord Macartney, with the full approval of the *Edinburgh Review*, commended his nation to the Court of China on the grounds that ' Englishmen never tried to disturb or dispute the worship and tenets of others . . . they come to China with no such views . . . they have no priests or chaplains with them as have other nations '.[1]

[1] Quoted in Coupland's *Wilberforce*.

PART THREE

1813–1857

PART III—1813–1857

CHAPTER VIII

PUBLIC OPINION AT HOME

Security of mission cause at home—significance of transfer of control to Parliament—growing support of missions—Mrs. Sherwood and Southey's *Life of Wesley*—activity of the Churches—influence of Liberalism.

IN tracing the development of the relations between missions and the Government during our next period, which extends from the 1813 Charter to the Mutiny of 1857, we can concentrate attention almost entirely on events in India. The British Parliament in securing for Christian missions the right of entry, and for the established church an episcopal representative in India, has played its part. We have now to see by what means and to what extent Christian missions won for their converts not merely toleration but protection and fair treatment, how far and in what ways they assisted and stimulated the civil authorities, in legislative, administrative, and educational spheres, to raise India morally and socially in accordance with Christian principles, and what they did to encourage a constitutionally timid Government to profess more openly the faith to which as trustee of a Christian nation it was pledged, and to realise that it was possible to tolerate all religions without slighting or repudiating the religion with which its name and greatness were associated. In the accomplishment of these tasks they relied mainly on their own efforts, and on sustaining the traditions of Schwartz and Carey. Their tact and universally recognised utility made frequent appeal to a higher authority at home unnecessary. They were conscious however throughout of an ever-growing body of public opinion in support of their claims throughout the British Isles. Their subordination to a chartered company had checked the full tide of free and generous British feeling. This check had been partially at least removed by subordination of the chartered company to popular representatives of the British realm.

It must not be supposed of course that the President of the Board of Control during this period abrogated his function of watchdog on behalf of the Government and the public conscience. Advised by his secret committee, and working through it, he was always there to see that the apprehensive Directors and occasionally evasive Governors-General remembered their position as trustees and their responsibility for the moral and intellectual improvement of India. When the time came for further renewal of the charter in 1833 and 1853 there was a thorough and useful overhauling and inventory by parliamentary committees. The charter of 1833 by terminating the commercial activities of the Company concentrated attention on their more edifying functions; by opening the trade of India to all, and by permitting residence free from restraint of licence to traders, planters, and missionaries alike, it subjected the Government of India to the independent, usually well-informed, and always alert criticism of non-official Europeans. The committee that preceded the charter of 1853[1] was perhaps the first body that paid special and careful attention to the evidence and recommendations of missionaries. The educational despatch of 1854, which established the present system of education in India, set its seal of approval on the work of Duff and Wilson, the missionary protagonists of the period, and was in

[1] The Commons' Committee of 1852 included Gladstone, Disraeli, Cobden and Macaulay. Peacock and J. S. Mill gave evidence before it.

many respects based on their advice.[1] And there are other occasions on which we shall find the home government intervening. But speaking generally we may say that the fight for Christian principles was fought, and fought successfully, in India.

Thackeray and Dickens, who never succeeded in penetrating what was at that time perhaps the somewhat unattractive surface of mission work, must not mislead us into supposing that there was in the British Isles any lively opposition to mission work during this period. The indifference and occasional antagonism that characterised the eighteenth century had given place to widespread and productive sympathy. The annual income of the C.M.S. and S.P.G. respectively rose from £1,300 and £800, in the first decade of the century, to £100,000 and £50,000 in 1850.[2] Dickens' obvious dislike of 'telescopic philanthropy' was probably due to what he regarded as a diversion of funds and interests from charity sorely needed at home to far distant objects. But it was no more true of that age than of any other that mission work reduced or impoverished benevolent enterprise at home.

For the cause of missions there was of course Mrs. Sherwood. A literary appreciation of *Little Henry and his Bearer* has yet to be attempted. Heber's hymn has more obvious literary merit and gained much money and support for the cause. Perhaps more effective among thoughtful and cultivated readers was Southey's *Life of John Wesley*, published in 1820. The Georgia work of

[1] The charter of Indian education, often referred to as the Wood despatch after Charles Wood (1st Viscount Halifax), who, as President of the Board of Control, prepared it in consultation with Duff, Wilson, and Trevelyan for despatch by the Directors.

[2] In 1825 only 5 per cent of the Scotch congregations responded to an appeal of the General Assembly for subscriptions. By 1837 the annual income was £7589.

John and Charles Wesley was indeed neither successful nor edifying. But Southey with supreme literary skill displayed the brothers as the virtual founders of all British mission work. No imaginative reader after realising from this work what these evangelists had achieved in heathen England of the eighteenth century could fail to see the possibilities of similar work among the 'inconvertible Hindus'. His judicious and tactful treatment of John Wesley's schismatic tendencies induced among the most devoted supporters of law and order a conviction that an 'enthusiast', whose inspiration was genuine and disinterested, was, with all his obvious dangers a source of life-giving power that no Church or country could afford to ignore or ridicule. From 1820 onwards 'enthusiasm' ceased to be in fact a term of reproach. Not all the credit for this must be attributed to John Wesley or his biographer. Carey and his fellow-Baptists had also shown in India that enthusiastic sectarians, even when drawn from the 'lower classes', can assist and strengthen established authority. If Wesley may by some be accused of strengthening in some respects that fear of reckless disregard for authority, which accounts for so much of the unpopularity of enthusiasm, the same charge cannot be laid to Carey's account. His initial landing and residence in India was, it is true, an act of defiance. But once there he adopted, rightly, a most conciliatory attitude towards the powers that be.

With the established church the growth of evangelical zeal from 1820 onwards was by no means confined to the evangelical section or to the followers of Simeon and Wilberforce. It was that party mainly that assisted the rapid growth of the C.M.S., but the high church party applied itself to the development of the Society for the Propagation of the Gospel which very early in this period extended its activities to India. The establishment of St. Augustine's College, Canterbury, reminds us that mission zeal transcended the bounds of church parties. And the dispatch of Alexander Duff[1] to India by the General Assembly of the Scotch Kirk symbolised the final abandonment by the established church of Scotland of its eighteenth-century attitude towards mission work.

Before we leave England for India we must not forget that the period under review is one in which the theories of Bentham were gradually being translated into administrative and legislative action. The work of men such as Bentinck and Dalhousie in India owed much to the support of public opinion that expressed itself in England through reforms quite as drastic and far-reaching as Bentinck's suppression of suttee or Dalhousie's Removal of Disabilities Act.[2] Duff and Wilson in their enthusiastic alliance with Macaulay and other devotees of 'useful information' and 'Western Sciences' felt behind them the moral support of Brougham and John Stuart Mill.

[1] In 1829. [2] See p. 132.

CHAPTER IX

BISHOPS, CHAPLAINS AND GOVERNORS-GENERAL IN INDIA HEBER, DUFF AND WILSON

The passing of Carey—the new area of controversy—two types of Governor-General—episcopal aims and influence—Heber's character and achievements—Daniel Wilson—official recognition of Christianity—stalwart Christians in the official world—the Lawrences, Edwardes, and Outram—their support of missions—merchants and chaplains.

THE protagonists of this period in India are the Scotsmen, Alexander Duff and John Wilson. Lesser stars in the firmament are the Anglican Heber and Daniel Wilson. There will be no more talk of William Carey. His pioneer work is over. But he was active and fruitful during the first half of our period and one great monument to his zeal will be unveiled when we study the significance of Serhampore College. There is much that is fascinating as well as much that is sad in the record of his last twenty years' work. But the tale of his persistence and his heroism in the face of opposition from home and tragic disaster in India is outside our subject. With him there passed away a man whose service had fulfilled the four conditions enumerated by Southey in his *Life of Wesley*. It had been hard, costly, and for many years forlorn and derided. In keeping open the door for Christian missions in India he had shown that the gift of the Holy Spirit, though always explosive, is not necessarily a danger to the existing and established order, and that a modern evangelist may imitate St. Paul, not only in his fervour but in his devoted and serviceable allegiance to a great Empire.

Led and inspired by him the Serhampore community, in addition to all their evangelical work, had laid the foundation of vernacular education, a vernacular press, and a vernacular prose literature in Bengal. From their own earnings they had built and endowed a college and set up the first steam printing-press in India. And they had undertaken the translation of the Bible into thirty-four languages. Nothing perhaps created a more favourable impression on the parliamentary committee of 1813 than the fact that Carey had devoted the substantial salary attached to his Fort William college post to the advancement of the mission. Despite the anxiety and disappointment of his later years in India there was much to gladden his heart, and, not least, the task that he undertook, as government translator, of rendering into Bengali the regulation of 1829 that put an end to suttee. We can well believe that the fact of the regulation reaching him on Sunday did not prevent him from assisting in the immediate publication of a reform for which he had worked so hard and long. In his last hours nothing more serious seems to have troubled him than a fear that after his death Brother Marshman would let the cows into his beloved garden. He was indeed 'seasoned timber'. There has perhaps been no missionary equal to him in India. There have been very few who have not been inspired by his example.

Against the Government of India hard words were often used during this period by men who were claiming for their native converts the same protection and rights that they had won for themselves as missionaries. It was not special privileges that they desired, but the same rights under the law and administrative regulations that were guaranteed expressly to adherents of all other religions in India. This, and perhaps a more open profession of the faith on which presumably authority relied in India as at home, was the substance of their frequent memorials and petitions.

Gradually and laboriously they secured one position after another. How slow the progress was may be estimated from the words of Bishop Heber in 1826. An ardent evangelist, he knew none the less the supreme need of tact and discretion. He recognised and testified to the moderation, wisdom, and essentially Christian foundations of our work in India at that time. But at the end of a long tour he records his deliberate conviction that 'we are surely in matters of religion the most lukewarm and cowardly people on the face of the earth' And he was on the point of putting his conviction emphatically before the Board of Control, with a demand for fair treatment of our fellow-Christians, when he died.

Heber would have been less contemptuous if he had lived to appreciate the resolute and straightforward policy of William Bentinck. Even the saintly Bishop Wilson, whose standard for Government was almost as high as that which he imposed on himself and his clergy, was unable to detect in him any fault except 'a strange dislike for Bishops'. This, even when combined with a lamentable 'absence of Church principles', could not condemn a ruler who defied Indian religious feeling, when it defended what was intolerable to a Christian conscience, and boldly stated that native Christians had the same claim to government employment and to legal protection of their civil rights as any other subjects of the realm. But not all his successors were so courageous.

In 1841 Alexander Duff, who was not slow to appreciate merit on the part of the Government nor fanatical in his judgment, publicly described the policy of Lord Auckland as 'remarkable for its concessions and compromises, for its education without religion, its ethics without a God'. His references to 'evasion and intrigue' in dealing with affairs of religion are frequent and emphatic. In answer to Duff's prayers and protests came Lord Dalhousie, from the right side of the border, with an irresistible love of fair play, and a sound conviction that it was not only our Christian duty but our wisest policy to show India that we were neither ashamed of being Christians nor afraid to protect them. In the troublous Mutiny period that ensued Dalhousie's wisdom was forgotten. Even at the close of our period, when the battle had been won, John Wilson, who had found the atmosphere of Bombay throughout more congenial to mission work than his fellow Scotsman Duff had found Bengal, shows great restraint and caution in his qualified commendation of the Government. 'Notwithstanding its sins and shortcomings it has not yet ventured to question *in any categorical form* the right of every Christian to support and promote the Christian religion'. The italicised words are significant. So too is the fact that such a defence was necessary nearly fifty years after the right of entry for Christian missions had been gained.

The fact that Bishop Heber was among those who protested against cowardice in high places reminds us that Parliament in 1813 had imposed on the Company a Bishop who was presumably to keep the authorities, as well as the chaplains, on the right path. It will be appropriate here to say something of the bishops' work as 'keepers of the Company's conscience'.

It was hardly to be expected that a Bishop of Calcutta whose see, up to 1833, included Ceylon and Australia as well as the whole of India, would find his time and energy equal to all the duties of his post. Critics of the episcopal scheme were in fact met by the retort that it was, like the criticised baby, 'only a little one'. One bishop and one archdeacon would not be expected to create any dangerous antagonism or to raise prematurely any awkward questions ; even the addition of a Presbyterian chaplain to the meagre establishment of each Presidency gave rise to little anxiety, and the most nervous critics were disarmed when the first Presbyterian chaplain announced openly that the conversion of the Hindu was in his opinion a hopeless task.

The see of Calcutta proved in fact a veritable death-trap. The extent, variety, and delicacy of the work, and the rigour of constant touring, under conditions far harder than those of to-day in every kind of climate, brought several careers of great promise to an abrupt close. The fact that seven bishops of Calcutta died at their posts between 1813 and 1833 was largely responsible for the substantial extension of the episcopal in the latter year.

Of the first bishop, Middleton[1], it may without injustice be said that he did not let the claims of Christian missions or their converts weigh heavily on him. Lord Teignmouth's prophesy that the episcopal invasion would be greeted with profound indifference was correct. When he landed in Calcutta, 'without eclat, so as to avoid any popular disturbance', 'the heart of India beat calmly as was its wont'. His wish to avoid any disturbance of the unruffled surface of India led to the emphatic dissociation of his office from the Bible Society and every form of mission work for a time. But disciplinary zeal made his relations to the Church of England missionaries a question of considerable anxiety and importance. 'These C.M.S. missionaries ! I must license or silence them !' The S.P.G. mission, as an official organ of the Church, presented less difficulty. His attitude to this mission, and the Bishops College scheme, after a letter of commendation from the Prince Regent, was almost

[1] Thomas Middleton, F.R.S. ; Prebendary of Lincoln ; first Bishop of Calcutta, 1814–1820.

cordial. But for the most part he was engaged, not ineffectively nor altogether unprofitably, in maintaining the dignity of his office and establishing an episcopal tradition. With a Presbyterian chaplain devoting much of his time to the claims of his church there were always questions of precedence that demanded painful attention. The comparative height of church steeples opened up a vast field of controversy. Of what use to the prestige of the Church of England was a higher steeple, if a weathercock, abnormally elevated with diabolical dexterity, proclaimed to every dawn the ultimate triumph of the Scotch Kirk !

No one could have adapted more skilfully the functions of the post to the Indian conception of what a Lord Padre Sahib ought to be. Here was dignity and repose and a genial atmosphere of 'Live and let live'. India liked its rulers to have their own Guru. It fitted in with their idea of sovereignty. The Government had its own priesthood, and it continued to administer with simple impartiality and wonderful efficiency the affairs of countless mosques and temples for which it was trustee ; it honoured the religious endowments which it had taken over from Hindu and Mohammedan predecessors as punctually as it paid the episcopal salary. Brahmin, moulvie, bishop, and archdeacon met on terms of perfect equality, all alike interested in questions affecting 'the establishment'. 'I too am a Brahmin', said a discredited but self-satisfied Raja to Bishop Heber, who had expressed surprise at the courtesy of his reception 'In token of his brotherly regard, he plucked some of his prettiest flowers for me.' Heber was approached more than once by Brahmins anxious to discuss with him the best methods of safeguarding common privileges. 'We must stand together', as the manager of a richly endowed temple remarked. During his many tours the episcopal cortege was often augmented and delayed by a following of suppliants, who threatened to die of starvation before his tent unless their demand for 'chits' of recommendation from the Governor-General's Guru was satisfied.

But Heber, during his all too short ministration, had time for other matters also. Without fear, and equally without indiscretion, he put evangelisation first among his many duties. His first task in visiting any station was to investigate, stimulate, and not seldom correct the local mission work. Many and important were his decisions. We shall come on traces of his work soon in the great questions of caste. He was president of the C.M.S. committee and called himself openly the first missionary of the Society. His prayer for the final conversion of the Raja of Tanjore, Schwartz's affectionate but not finally secured pupil, was circulated for use in all Anglican places of worship. It is surprising and creditable to the authorities that in an age when they were, according to Heber, so 'cowardly and lukewarm' they should have tolerated without a protest such action on the part of one with whom they were so closely associated. Probably they understood and appreciated the discretion with which Heber's zeal was always tempered. There was nothing of the fanatic in him. He regarded the maintenance of the British empire as essential for the evangelisation of India. And nothing, not even the prohibition of such a ghastly business as suttee, could be approved if it involved a risk to that Empire. He was far from sharing the view of the British official who optimistically described the procedure as 'a light affliction working for the widows an exceeding weight of glory'. But, like so many of his contemporaries he underrated the Indian respect for strength allied with justice. Our Indian Empire, he thought, was in imminent danger and could be sustained only by official deference to all old-established customs. His orders against street preaching were precise and emphatic. We are left wondering what St. Paul's reply would have been to such orders from Jerusalem. We know what the Roman official thought and did, and the wholesome fear inspired at Ephesus by his orders. It was perhaps the Government more than Heber that deserved reproach for cowardice.

The other great Bishop of the period, Daniel Wilson, during the many years of his episcopate, followed Heber in his zealous care for missionary work. Like him too he was both fearless and discreet. But he was not like him over-anxious for the security of our Empire. Perhaps he was familiar with Dryden's great words, 'I have heard indeed of some virtuous persons who have ended unfortunately, but never of any virtuous nation ; Providence is engaged too deeply when the cause becomes so general'. Acting on the principle that 'Righteousness exalteth a nation' he was constant in admonition when he thought unmeaning concessions were made to timidity. He placed more than one official rebuff to his credit, and we shall find him foremost among those who openly attacked the exclusion of the Bible from Government schools.

Men of the calibre of Heber and Daniel Wilson, backed by the authority of the Church and firmly entrenched in a position secured by public opinion at home and the express will of Parliament, could not fail to leave their mark on the Government of India. They were ably backed by chaplains, such as Thomason and Corrie, who owed their original inspiration to Simeon, and were worthy successors to Daniel Brown and Claudius Buchanan. So far indeed as outward observance of religion and reasonable provision for adequate and decent ministration to Europeans were concerned the bishop and his establishment cannot have found their task difficult. Bentinck and Dalhousie were not men who were likely to forget, among their manifold duties, the respect that the Government owed to the Christian religion. Even Lord Ellenborough, whose nervous preoccupation with the explosive potentialities of all religion will engage our attention later, was punctilious in his official recognition of the necessity for divine assistance. After the victorious campaign against the Afghans in 1842 he reminded the official world in a dignified proclamation of 'the duty of humble thanksgiving to Almighty God imposed on us all, and of prayer that we may not abuse His bounty and that we may be made fit instruments for the government of the great nation which His wisdom has placed under British rule'. At the beginning of our period the construction of 'a few cheap chapels' seemed to the Directors all that was required for the purpose of the modest establishment imposed on them by Parliament. But, though a Christian government in India had never even tried to rival the pious munificence of its Hindu and Mohammedan predecessors, the period as a whole is one of considerable activity in church building. And from 1833 onwards the establishment of chaplains was substantially increased and the Directors' tendency to save money by long delay in the falling of vacancies was corrected. The principle enunciated by Heber at the beginning of the period was effectively impressed by Dalhousie on the official world before its close. The Hindu and Mohammedan communities found it easier to respect a Government which made decent provision for its own religion. Such provision showed that their rulers were not only strong and resolute but also human and generous. And these are characteristics dear to the Indian world.

The Government, in so far as it was determined to profess and call itself Christian, and we shall have to note later on the restrictions imposed by timidity or inevitable conditions on this resolve, found at its disposal many of its servants who were eager to co-operate. Of Anglo-Indian society generally we shall have more to say later. The evidence is conflicting. But testimony is unanimous as to the stalwart and manifest Christianity of such men as the Lawrences, James Outram, Herbert Edwardes, Mountstuart Elphinstone, Robert Grant, and James Thomason, Bartle Frere, Montgomery, McLeod, and Thornton, Muir and Durand.

All these and others, most of them Governors or Commissioners of Provinces, proved themselves 'bold, independent and yet Christian rulers, uncrowned kings of men by grace and election'.[1] 'They considered themselves Governors-General at least', is typical of the criticism urged against them. Many of their actions indeed seem even at the present day bold and uncompromising. To the supreme authorities, with their fear of popular disturbance, they were often most embarrassing. But there was nothing soft or sentimental in their composition. Their respect for law and order as imperial aims was Pauline in its intensity. Their will was indeed law and in few areas where they had predominated was there any serious trouble in 1857. Hindu and Mohammedan alike were confident that men who advocated their own religion with such transparent honesty were honest also in their undertaking to protect all religious practices that were harmless to the community as a whole.

'Methodism at home is no unprofitable game. In the East it will soon be the infallible road to promotion.' The prophetic grumbler in the *Edinburgh Review* of 1808 was right. But the methodism that triumphed in the men who consolidated our Indian possessions and retained them for us in 1857 was a quality of character

[1] Contemporary verdict quoted in Smith's *Twelve Indian Statesmen.*

not the snuffling cant which is wrongly connected with the term. Lawrence and Edwardes were bound to 'get on' not because they were 'Methodists', they were in fact orthodox Churchmen, but because of their clear grasp of essential principles and their courage in applying them. 'We are much safer', said Edwardes, at a time when men's hearts were failing them for fear, 'if we do our duty, than if we neglect it.' 'We must endeavour solely', wrote John Lawrence to the Government of India, 'to ascertain what is our Christian duty and follow that to the uttermost, undeterred by any consideration. . . . Christian things done in a Christian way will never alienate the heathen.' And later he pleaded for open avowal of Christian intentions 'so that the people may see that we have no sinister or sudden designs'.

Such men were openly interested in the work of evangelisation and regardless of the disapproval and mistrust that such interest inspired in their superiors and subordinates alike. Shortly after the advance to Peshawar Colonel Mackenson, who was in charge of the recently acquired area, announced that no missionary should cross the Indus while he was commissioner. 'Do you want us all to be killed?' he said to a major who represented the mission. A few weeks later he was murdered by an Afghan. Edwardes, his successor, approached by the same representatives, replied, 'Certainly! send for a missionary, call a meeting and I will preside'. The date fixed for the meeting was also set apart for a steeplechase. Refusing any postponement on this account, in his opening speech he enlarged on the need for a mission not to the minds and bodies but to the souls of men and emphasised the claim that missionaries of all religions had on the protection of Government. In the face of ridicule and opposition he proceeded. One of his subordinates derisively subscribed a rupee towards a revolver for the first missionary. But Pfander,[1] who preached and argued openly in the most fanatic areas of Peshawar throughout the Mutiny, needed no revolver. There was that in Edwardes that endeared him to a man like Ruskin, who has left his impressions of him in 'a Knight's Quest'. Donald McLeod, who rose to the Lieut.-Governorship of the Punjab, as a junior officer in a remote district in 1833 recorded officially his view that our deeds, by which he referred to the government patronage of idolatry, must be viewed at the throne of God as deserving of divine vengeance. James Thomason, who reached similar rank, openly worshipped with converts of humble rank, translated the Psalms into Hindustani, and announced, while opening a government college in his official capacity as head of a province, that he looked forward hopefully to the christianisation of India. He took a leading part in the foundation of the mission college in Agra and proved himself in every way the son of the devout chaplain and godson of Simeon.

We read of a Governor of Bombay who held a Sunday school class. Attendance of officials at the public baptism of converts and at public disputation between missionaries and pandits was not uncommon. At a time when public feeling in Bombay was exasperated a police commissioner on his own responsibility safeguarded the baptism of six Parsee converts. A memorial to the C.M.S. urging intensive work in Bombay was signed by a Commissioner of Scinde, sixteen civilians of high standing and twenty-three military officers. 'Arise, for this matter belongeth unto thee. We also will be with thee.'

In Bombay particularly, but in other parts to a less degree, government servants contributed liberally to missions. We find military officers in the British Army

[1] Representative of the C.M.S.

urging privates and non-commissioned officers to subscribe. The victorious army in the Punjab raised a subscription for the C.M.S. as a thanksgiving. Residents in native states such as Nagpur, Assam and Kathiawar invited missions to establish settlements. The Political Commissioner of Baroda accompanied John Wilson, when he expounded the Christian faith to the Gaekwar, and 'took the chair' when he argued with the Court pandit. The Gaekwar was kind enough to congratulate Wilson on his Marathi accent. As for himself, his business was with this world, not the next. But he was pleased to accept the gift of a Bible through the Political Commissioner. For their interest in his welfare he thanked this intelligent Padre and his commissioner colleague. So different from the Lord Padre Sahib 'who always asks to see the artillery'.

The Bayard of India, Outram, was fearless in religion and in war alike. Convinced that our past war policy in Scinde was radically unjust, he offered his prize-money to Lord Ellenborough as compensation to the dispossessed Amirs of the land. A Gibbon would show us the apprehensive Proconsul applauding the chivalry, but deploring the enthusiasm, of the action. His actual words are, perhaps fortunately, not recorded. The prize-money was eventually handed over by Outram, as the price of blood, to a Christian mission.

Stouthearted merchants too were not found wanting. In 1845 they gave Duff £1000 for his Calcutta work. And there were Government chaplains whom no episcopal caution could restrain from mission work. Thomason and Corrie, usually known as 'the black chaplains', remembered the instructions given to the Company's pastors in 1698, and were able to give some of their best to India without stinting their European ministrations. Another chaplain, James Grey[1] 'of

[1] For further account see Smith's *Life of John Wilson*.

Bhooj', devoted the last four years of his life to the edification of the raja of that principality and his Gujarati subjects. It was under his influence that slavery and infanticide were suppressed within the State. There was something of a Schwartz about him. A shoemaker at the outset of his life, friend of Burns, correspondent of Wordsworth, contributor to *Blackwood*, and persevering orientalist, he has strangely failed to win a place in the *Dictionary of National Biography*.

CHAPTER X

ADVANCE ON CHRISTIAN LINES BENTINCK AND DALHOUSIE

Significance of Bentinck and Dalhousie—their supporters—suppression of suttee—campaign against superstitious malpractices—Thuggee and infanticide—remarriage of widows—slavery and the penal code—the civil rights and status of Indian Christians—schools for Christian sepoys—marriage of Indian converts—the conversion of minors—treatment and employment of outcastes—opposition to employment of Christians.

THE individual efforts of men such as we have described in the preceding chapter must not be regarded as embodying the explicit policy of a responsible Government. We shall have indeed to record later the periodic attempts of that Government to curb their enthusiasm and to discountenance any idea that the Government as such took any interest in the evangelisation of India. But the clear convictions of such agents encouraged and assisted Bentinck and Dalhousie to assert, against determined opposition, the rights of native Christians and to advance on Christian lines by legislation and administrative action the moral and social condition of India.

We must not exaggerate the enterprise of these two rulers. The good work had been begun by Cornwallis and Wellesley ; during Bentinck's regime John Malcolm in the west and Thomas Munro in the south were showing equal determination, though in a more limited sphere. Bentinck, and to a lesser extent Dalhousie, could count on the wholehearted support of a Parliament that was still inspired and animated by the Reform Act of 1832. That the end of all government is the good of all the governed was the slogan of the times. The first factory act for children, the first annual state grant for education, and the final abolition of slavery were the English accompaniment to Bentinck's humanitarian theme. The missionaries and the bishops were shrewd enough to see the importance of more rapid and frequent communication between England, with its new sense of responsibilities, and benighted India. They took the lead in urging upon the P. and O. Company and Government the importance of the overland route. Duff and Wilson were always at hand to support and substantiate episcopal representations. Bentinck created quite a sensation by inviting Duff to a Government House reception. And last, but not least, there was a small but very solid phalanx of Indian reformers, led by Ram Mohun Roy, to stimulate and reassure Bentinck in all his most daring work.

But, when all have received the honour due to them, the work of Bentinck and Dalhousie remains as an enduring monument of brave and resolute achievement. Bentinck was not faultless, Apart from his strange dislike of bishops and an established church, he is reproached by one contemporary with 'writing as many minutes as all his predecessors put together', while another says that 'he muddled what he meddled with as often as he improved it'. But few would deny that he earned the inscription written by Macaulay for his statue in Calcutta. 'He inspired Oriental despotism with the spirit of Britain and freedom, his constant study was to elevate the moral and intellectual character of the Government committed to his charge.' No less a tribute could justly be paid to Dalhousie. Neither of these two men ever forgot the constant need for tactful toleration of all forms of religion. But in each the question how far a Christian government ought to tolerate what it knows to be morally wrong was constantly introducing itself. There were many evils that seemed to them outside the sphere of direct gove nment action. Child marriage, certain gross forms of polygamy, and the widespread use of divorce, seemed to many western and oriental minds then, as they seem to-day, prolific of evil. But they left them to the influence of enlightened and informed public opinion. There remained many gross practices connected with the religions of the country which they shrank from 'perpetuating with a new authority by leaving them untouched', though to touch them might be construed as violation of their pledged impartiality.

First and foremost among them came suttee, the immolation of widows on their dead husbands' pyres. The horror and popularity of this practice had been reported by many since William Carey submitted his report. Though none denied that it was often a signal proof of voluntary devotion and piety (Sleeman reports such a case in the Central Provinces long after suttee had become illegal and it is not unknown to-day)[1] there was abundant evidence of its being encouraged or even enforced by men who under cover of religion were seeking to evade the expense of maintaining the widows or to secure for themselves their property. Albuquerque's refusal to countenance it in Portuguese India may or may not have been known to Bentinck. That Metcalfe and Bayley had prohibited it in the areas of their administration was known to him, as was also the ruling of certain Hindu lawyers that the Shastras enjoined on widows the alternatives of chastity *or* immolation, and the fact that there was no universally accepted Hindu authority for insisting on either alternative. He was assured by Ram Mohun Roy[2] that there would be no general uprising. With this support he rejected the ingenuous defence by a subordinate of this 'exceeding

[1] See list of authorities, s.v.

[2] Hindu reformer, see p. 171.

light affliction ', he refused to accept as adequate the existing regulations that ' notice of intention should be sent to the nearest police officer ', which obviously implicated the Government in the sin ; he turned in despair from the ' Orientalists ' who combined with their very legitimate love of the Hindu classics an exaggerated belief in their hold on the multitudes ; and on a certain Sunday in 1829 he sent William Carey, Bengali translator to Government, his order suppressing suttee throughout British India. There was much agitation and clamour which culminated in an appeal rejected by the Privy Council in 1832. But there was no disturbance of a serious nature. The practice survived in many native states up to 1847 when Lord Hardinge commented on its suppression in Kashmir, and added significantly that he abstained from publishing the names of those states that had not yet taken such action, as he confidently expected that they would soon do ! Within the next ten years it became illegal all over India.

Other forms of human sacrifice had been attacked by the authorities before suttee ; Wellesley, on Carey's report, had made the dedication of children to the sacred waters at Saugor Point, and the exposure of the aged on the banks of the Ganges, penal offences. The campaign against similar manifestations of piety continued intermittently throughout the period. It was most intensive in the time of Lord Hardinge. From 1850 onwards human sacrifice has persisted only in remote areas among the most primitive tribes.

Thuggee was another evil that had spread widely over large tracts of India and was associated in the popular mind with religion. The thieves who waylaid travellers and strangled them after entering into friendly talk were devotees of Bhawani or Kali, wife of Siva. They had religious ceremonies of their own in which the sacramental consumption of sugar played a part. This aspect of their work is admirably shown in some of Meadows Taylor's books.[1] Bentinck, though not the first to make war against them, surpassed all his predecessors in the rigour and success of his methods ; superintended by the ubiquitous and indefatigable Sleeman, the Thuggee department effected the conviction of over 1500 Thugs between 1826 and 1835. By the time Bentinck left India Thuggee as a religious organisation had practically ceased to exist, though highway robbery on similar lines necessitated the maintenance of a Thuggee and dacoity department in some parts of Central India until recent times.

Infanticide in India from the beginning of history has been a practice recognised and tacitly approved among certain castes and communities. The last census report (1921) suggests distinctly its survival in parts of North India. Jonathan Duncan had suppressed it in Benares and parts of western India before the time of Bentinck. From 1830 onwards the areas in which it was explicitly condemned and treated as criminal were steadily extended. In Central India, among the Rajput states and elsewhere the struggle was particularly severe. We hear of a ruler of Rajkot who was sequestrated in 1835 as accessory to the murder of an infant daughter in defiance of an agreement made some years before between the British representative and a group of local Rajas.[2] They had bound themselves to outcaste any of their community found guilty of a crime that was stated in the bond to be contrary to the teaching of the Shastras. Dalhousie took steps to have the practice definitely and publicly notified as murder in all parts of India.

The hard fate of Hindu widows has been a constant theme of humanitarian writers from the earliest times

[1] See particularly *Confessions of a Thug*, 1839. Taylor served for many years in Hyderabad and Berar.

[2] See Aitchison's *Sanads and Treaties*, vol. iv, 422.

up to the present day. The degradation and hardship to which they are subjected under cover of religious sentiment cannot be cured by any legislative or administrative measures. But Dalhousie in passing the Act of 1856 which legalised their remarriage was advancing on the humanitarian lines laid down when his predecessor suppressed suttee.

We may pass quickly by the other humanitarian measures which adorned this period. For the evils against which they were aimed and the sentiment which inspired them are not directly associated with any form of religion. Such measures may perhaps justly be called Christian in so far as they have been carried through with least opposition and greatest speed in Christian lands or by Governments that profess themselves Christians. For this reason they are mentioned here. But they involve no subordination of one religion to another and are the outcome of an upward ethical tendency rather than of any distinct change in man's attitude towards God or the unseen world.

Slavery was recognised in India up to the time of Bentinck. The revenue department for instance in selling the property of a defaulter included his slaves among the property to be sold. Slave traffic between district and district was prohibited in 1832. The charter of 1833 naturally provided for the mitigation and ultimate abolition of the status. In 1843 legal recognition was finally denied to it. Barbaric modes of punishment, including branding, which had been taken over from our predecessors, had disappeared by 1849. The Indian Penal Code, begun by Macaulay and completed just after the close of the period, was one of its chief humanitarian triumphs. The custody of lunatics was regularised on humaner lines ; lepers continued to be outcastes liable to most savage treatment, if we may trust the accounts of men such as Duff who saw or heard of them being buried alive. Bentinck, in 1834, abolished the penalty of flogging in the Indian Army ; but this was condemned even by enlightened critics as premature. Comic papers of the period refer satirically to its retention among white troops after it had been found unseemly for sepoys :

> 'For Christian backs remaining still
> A moral source of every ill' ;

and the measure was before long rescinded.

But it is now time for us to turn to measures calculated to secure equality of rights for native Christians. And first among these must be placed Dalhousie's great Act of 1850 which firmly established for all British India the great principle that a man's religion should not operate in such a way as to deprive him of his civil rights. There was no explicit reference to Christianity in the measure, but it was generally recognised that its main result was to secure Christian converts from loss of property and of rights of inheritance. Under Hindu and Mohammedan law apostasy was penalised by loss of all such rights. And Warren Hastings had pledged the British Government to the observance and maintenance of those parts of the pre-existing laws and customs which touched directly on religion. Ostensibly for this reason, and also no doubt because the setting aside of this penalty removed one of the most powerful obstacles to conversion, there was a widespread and intensive agitation against the bill. Special stress was laid on the ceremonial responsibilities incurred by inheritors. Was a son for instance to be relieved by 'perversion' of the annual ceremonies on which the propitiation of his father's spirit depended and yet to remain in possession of property inherited from the father ? Dalhousie stoutly emphasised the distinction between ceremonial and legal responsibility, asserted the inalienable right of the supreme Government to regulate succession to property, and maintained that, when two pledges were inconsistent, the wider and more general must prevail. A Government that had promised to tolerate all religions could not be restrained from securing justice for one religion by a pledge to respect the legal rights of any other religions. Here again it was Bentinck who initiated the reform by a regulation of 1832 which seems to have been confined to Bengal. The bishop of Bombay in 1845 drew the Government's attention to the loss inflicted on converts in his diocese. Legislation was attempted and abandoned in response to agitation. A further memorial from the bishop followed and it was left for Dalhousie to establish legally and universally a principle for which Bentinck and a bishop (philanthropy acquaints a man with strange bed-fellows) had done so much.

On similar grounds Dalhousie, as head of the administration, swept aside all objections to the supply of Christian instruction for the children of native Christians in the Company's troops. Though as we shall see later native Christians were in fact if not in theory rejected from the Bengal Army, there were in other parts, and especially in south India, regiments where native Christians were sufficiently strong and numerous to make their claims in this important matter audible in high quarters.

The problems connected with the marriage of Christian converts were even more important and far more complicated. On the ecclesiastical side they had caused Heber and Daniel Wilson many anxious moments. What was the correct course for instance when a convert had several wives, attached to himself in unenlightened days, dependent on him? Both bishops were inclined to follow when possible the instructions of St. Paul, though with some inward misgivings apparently as to the infallibility of his authority where women were concerned. It seemed safe, even though it might be a little callous, to retain only the first wife. But temporal precedence was perhaps not a safe guide where some wives followed the faith of the husband and some did not. It was all very perplexing. On the civil side such subtleties demanded less attentions. An important step was taken when converts were freed from all legal obligations to Hindu wives united only by child marriage, or to wives who refused for a stated period to join their husbands after conversion. Christian marriage was given civil and legal status during the period. But several other questions remained unsettled till after the close of the period.

Many bitter controversies, sometimes culminating in riots, arose out of the question as to the age at which a minor may be considered to have attained such discretion as justifies acceptance of a faith other than that of the parents without parental permission. The policy among missionaries during the period seems to have varied ; Duff in Bengal seems to have regarded at times the attainment of fourteen years as qualification for independent judgment, while in Bombay Wilson apparently considered sixteen a safer age. Much depended obviously on local and personal circumstances ; but there can be no doubt that some of the cases brought before the courts displayed bitter hostility to conversion as such rather than a *bona fide* desire to protect youth. In Calcutta Duff had several hard battles to fight, one of which ended in a challenge to a duel, sent to Duff by a European barrister whose public denunciation of missions for their 'unfair' campaign against immature boys was ruthlessly and with equal publicity investigated by the stalwart Scotsman. In Bombay the conversion in 1839 of three Parsees, between sixteen and twenty years of age, led to riots, lawsuits, the formation of an anti-mission league, and the submission of a Parsee memorial to the Directors. The memorialists protested against mission schools, urged that converts should not only lose their property and rights of inheritance, but also continue to be responsible for the families that were to be taken from them, and prayed that the 'age of discretion' should legally be fixed at twenty-one. The Bombay Government and Government of India took a commendably strong line on the memorial and recommended a continuance of strict neutrality and a fresh issue of Bentinck's regulation providing equal rights and privileges for all. The memorial met with little support from other communities or other localities in India and was wisely disregarded by the Directors.

The courts in dealing with such delicate cases showed on the whole no bias during the period, though in the earlier years there was perhaps a tendency to show exaggerated respect for the rights of parents. This was in any case a fault on the right side. By the close of the period the general principle seems to have been established by Sir Henry Maine[1] and other jurists that it was for judges to decide, with reference to the special circumstances of each case, what age, if any, short of sixteen, might reasonably be regarded as an age of discretion. It was clearly not a question that permitted any statutory definition.

The employment by Government of natives of India in positions of authority brought into consideration the rights of various castes and creeds to such employment. This question, which brings us into a sphere where religious prejudice plays a large part, became acute only in Bentinck's time. Cornwallis, in organising the Civil Service, had differentiated natives from Europeans and made it clear that parts of real responsibility would fall only to the latter. But Bentinck's regulation of 1832, declaring that no one should be disqualified from

[1] Legal member of Governor-General's Council, 1862–1869.

office on grounds of religion, birth, descent, or colour, was incorporated in the parliamentary charter of 1833. Out of this clause in the Charter came the pronouncement of 1835 in favour of a western education, that would fit the natives for posts from which they were no longer debarred, and for which indeed they were, in the interests of economy, sorely needed. But the clause also raised questions of great delicacy. No previous rulers of India had hesitated to give preference to members of particular castes or adherents of particular religions in distributing the sweets of office. If Hindus succeeded in gaining high office under the later Mohammedan rulers, they owed their success to their merits and to their skill in proving their peculiar usefulness rather than to any abstract principle of justice or equality.

On the whole it may be said of the British Government that with one exception they carried out loyally and to the best of their ability during this period the intention of this declaration. If the Brahmins continued, as under our predecessors, to obtain a share of office out of all proportion to their numbers, it was due to their skill in absorbing western education and not to any favouritism on the Government's part. If at times Mohammedans were preferred to more competent Hindus the choice denoted a desire to see both religions fairly represented in office rather than any partiality for Islam. The question of employing outcastes, which touched the Hindu on his most sensitive point, hardly emerged during the period as the educational attainments which Government required of candidates rarely if ever fell to the lot of those unfortunates.

A certain lack of firmness in demanding for such outcastes admission into schools controlled by Government was indeed noticeable and will be discussed in another context. But the one important exception to the principle of equality enunciated in the charter of

1833 was the Government's treatment, not of outcastes, but of native Christians. Converts, so far as government office was concerned, soon came to understand that profession of the same religion as their rulers, far from being regarded as a qualification for office, actually disqualified them and served as excuse for violating the spirit of the equality clause in the charter. It is with this subject that we shall now begin our study of that side of our rule in India which is less creditable to our reputation as protectors of all forms of religion.

CHAPTER XI
REACTIONARY INFLUENCE

European society in India—conditions of life—literary evidence—Mrs. Sherwood, W. D. Arnold and Miss Eden—intellectual and spiritual atrophy—periodical literature—Auckland and the Peregrine Maitland case—Government patronage of idolatry—our polytheistic liabilities—dry nurse to Vishnu—Ellenborough and the Somnath gates—ecclesiastical and lay protest—Directors intervene—ambiguity and delay—home feeling supports gradual withdrawal from temple management—recognition of caste by government and missions—Bishop Wilson's firmness—support of missions by Government servants—ambiguous warnings—encourage suspicion—converts in Bengal army—the case of Prabhu Din Naick.

THE preceding account of what the Government of India during this period was able to accomplish in accordance with Christian principles and for the protection of Christian converts was introduced by a reference to the large and distinguished band of capable and resolute government officers who did not hesitate openly to proclaim their allegiance to the Christian faith and their determination to secure fair play for it. Tribute was paid to their influence in the policy of the Government. Men such as Dalhousie and Bentinck were encouraged to proceed resolutely on lines congenial to themselves. The more timid rulers were often embarrassed and sometimes spurred into action by their vitality.

But there was another side to European life in India. Rulers who wanted support for inaction or pusillanimity never failed to find it among some of the types of European Society presented to us by the literature and letters of the period. It was indeed hardly to be expected that the wave of reform that was steadily sweeping away abuses and cleansing public life in England should perform so effectively its ‘priestlike task’ in India during this period. Means of communication between the two countries, thanks largely to the efforts of Wilson and Duff, were greatly improved before the period ended. But they remained inadequate to secure that interplay of thought and feeling which vitalises life in India to-day. Leave in Europe was seldom taken. Mind and body were seldom refreshed by residence in the Hills. There was little to relieve the ‘hot dull vacancy of Indian life’. The taunt of those days that men left their morals behind them at the Cape was far less true of this period than of that which preceded it. But there seems to have been little of general interest or culture that survived the first few years of service. A station dinner in the 'forties must have been indeed a dull affair. One can hardly imagine any sprightly scheme for the moral or spiritual advance of India emerging from the evening drive round the Maidan that followed it. The station club in India to-day still remains fair game for the satirist. But it has at least its books and papers only a fortnight late; and there are always new-comers fresh from leave and, in the cold weather, visitors to remind its members of interests and ideas in the larger world.

‘There is a spirit of hostility to true holiness among the majority of our countrymen which threatens to have an outbreak.’ This is strong condemnation from John Wilson who weighed his words, mixed freely with all classes of Bombay society, and was quick to recognise the kindly and active interest that some of its members showed in his work. The atmosphere in Bombay was always more favourable to mission work than in Bengal. Commerce was on the whole less suspicious than officialdom, and Hindu caste or Islam's sensitiveness were not so obtrusive in west India as the Bengal authorities found them. Regarding life in east India Mrs. Sherwood is even more uncompromising. In her Indian version of *Pilgrim's Progress,* Vanity Fair owes much of its meretricious glitter to European thoughtlessness or worse. 'He that spake of the cross was despised in that street.' Little Henry, who at the age of seven is quite sure he 'could not find one good person in all the market', has frequent reminders that sin is not confined to one colour. His step-mother 'always employed herself at table (when not actually eating) in smoking her hookah and most of her visitors did the same; instead of pleasant and useful discourse there was in general nothing to be heard but the rattling of plates and knives and forks, the creaking of a large fan suspended from the ceiling and the gurgling of water in the pipes'; a little variety was gained by scolding the servants and calling them names in their own language.

Mrs. Sherwood's standard was high and her outlook perhaps restricted, though she was a shrewd observer and practised what she preached. The impressions of a cultured and conscientious Punjab civilian, free from all prejudice or religious sectarianism, are equally depressing. W. D. Arnold[1] was far from happy in society which has left its mark on the novel dedicated by him to its exposure. *Oakfield* is an honest record of a brave struggle against uncongenial surroundings; as a sombre picture of India in the 'forties it is entitled to respect and in places to praise. But as a whole it is the dullest work that has ever emerged from a family of literary distinction. It is to be hoped that Matthew was not flippant about it. There is no record that he ever read it to the end.

The hero of *Oakfield* finds his first experiences of life in India 'most disappointing and often shocking'. Looking back on the society he had known there he

[1] Son of Dr. Arnold, 1828–1859; military officer in civil employ; Director of Public Instruction in the Punjab. His early death on journey home is commemorated by Matthew Arnold in *A Southern Night*.

finds it 'shallow, empty, and contemptible'. In vain does he urge his neighbours to 'think something, hope something, look forward to something'. Wherever he looks he is presented with a universal blank, finding everywhere 'an utter want of nobleness'. The official bears the mark of his commercial origin. Entangled in 'a gross and degrading mechanism', with no counteracting influence such as piety or philosophy provide in England, 'he views a large portion of God's world as a profitable investment'. His indictment of 'the young fop of eighteen, product of the half-school, half-college system of Haileybury', who arrived in India quite unfit to fight against its evil genius, reminds us that Fort William College, as devised by Wellesley for the training of such men as Thomason and Metcalfe, had come to an end in 1830. No respect for abstract ideas, no serious insight into life, no recognition of spiritual facts, can anywhere be found. 'Shiploads of courage, bushels of pure unselfish visionary enthusiasm' are required before the foundations of Christianity can be established. Missionaries are useless. With Anglo-Indian Society as it is, Christianity can spread over India only like a mere superficial fashion of speech.

The Government resembles the society whose members determine its policy. No one short of a philosopher king can breathe into it that 'nobility' for which India looks. Its outlook is wholly secular. Whereas there is in most civilised countries a partially recognised idea of the higher and more spiritual ends of government, Calcutta looks solely to the protection of life and property and revenue collection. Few if any governments have been so just and liberal. None has ever been less inspired. We are reminded again and again, as we read the indictment, of the Roman Empire under Trajan. There must indeed have been many a Pliny who would have been the better for reading this antidote to self-satisfaction. But it is doubtful whether Paul ever cherished such resentment against the powers that be, ordained of God, to whom he owed the facilities that made his great task possible. Honour to whom honour is due! Arnold, as an official, may have been reluctant to defend himself. It is a common failing among Englishmen in India. It is sometimes said that intercourse between Indian and European was easier and less restrained in those days when communication with Europe was more difficult and when Anglo-Indian Society was thrown more completely on the resources of the country. If this was indeed the case a livelier interest in India's social and moral progress might reasonably have been expected. But in the Punjab as Arnold saw it the two races lived in different and irreconcilable worlds. Or, as Miss Eden put it, 'Queen Adelaide and O'Connell, the Jerseys and Pembrokes, are not further apart and more antipathetic than European and Native'.

Miss Eden, depicting the social world from its centre at Government House, though lighter in heart and touch than the sombre Punjab civilian, gives us an equally depressing picture of its intellectual barrenness. This clever good-natured woman of the world, 'dead and buried and sitting in her hot grave' in Calcutta, or visiting upcountry stations with her brother the Governor-General, Lord Auckland, notes in the late 'thirties of last century the complete absence of 'topics of interest indigenous to the soil' and the ineffective substitution of endless local gossip. English books are scarcely obtainable, though the success of *Pickwick* was such that there was an early reprint of it, lithographs and all, in Calcutta; 'the only bit of fun in India'.

Her visitors in Calcutta are merely on their way out to make their fortune, or on their way home because they have made it, or because their health requires change of station and they come here to ask for it. The new arrivals sometimes stagger us (with their complexions), but we simply say, 'How coarse' and wait with confidence for the effects that three weeks' baking will have. Among her European acquaintances she finds not one pleasing or accomplished woman, 'not the sixth part of one'. Nothing vitalises a society composed of 'the smallest macadamized gossips' who 'sneer at each other's dresses and looks, and pick out small stories against each other by means of the Ayahs'. Despite the recognised existence of 'various native Mrs. Aides-de-Camp', profligacy is almost unknown. Husband and wife drive out perforce together because the society of neither is desired elsewhere. There is nothing to sap the morality of an Indian station. But on a foundation of 'low spirits and constant *tracasseries*' nothing of beauty or use can effectively be built.

It is doubtful whether Government House just at this time did much to raise the general tone of society, which was so sharply criticised by one of its inmates.

'George[1] says the Directors occasionally write a fine sentence about not attending exclusively to British interests, just as if the British were here for any other purpose, or as if everybody's interest were not to keep the country at peace.' There is a note of vulgarity in the prelude and a plausibility in its close that must have characterised much of the dinner talk at this period. Duff finds its exposure necessary in an admirably frank denunciation of Lord Auckland's whole policy. It was often too much for the Lawrences and Elphinstones of the period to counter. Such men however received valuable support from the journals which began during this period to enlighten Calcutta and extend the sphere of Anglo-Indian interests. The press remained unfettered throughout, and in the weekly *Friend of India*

[1] Lord Auckland. Quoted from Miss Eden's letters. See list of authorities, s.v.

(1833), *Quarterly Calcutta Review* (1844), and daily *Harkaru*, missionaries such as Duff and Marshman, civil servants such as Henry Lawrence, and Army officers such as Marsh and Kaye dealt with general questions of the day in a fearless, intelligent, and Christian spirit.

A topic that excited frequent and painful controversy in papers such as these, as well as in missionary periodicals and occasionally in Parliament, was the official attitude of the Government towards idolatry and the more obviously reprehensible practices of Islam and Hinduism. 'What mischief religion does in a country', Miss Eden writes plaintively in 1837. 'George' found it most vexatious that 'an unsensible person like Sir Peregrine Maitland should refuse to give the national festivals the usual honours of drums, guns, etc., which they have had ever since the English set foot in India'. How tiresome was this 'irritation kept up on the plea of conscience when the soothing system would be much more commendable and much easier'!

It was indeed a troublesome budget of papers that had come from Madras to the Governor-General, Lord Auckland, already perplexed, and the hot weather beginning too, with difficulties about the opium trade with China and the Afghan frontier. For the stricter sect of Christian officials was in revolt. A memorial against official patronage of idolatry, signed by two hundred representatives of the ecclesiastical, civil, and military departments and of the non-official world, had been submitted through Bishop Corrie to the Madras Government, who had thereupon censured the Bishop for 'not moderating the zeal of overheated minds'. Bishops are not censured publicly every day. And this Bishop had heaped more fuel on the fire by appealing against the censure to the Governor-General, and by dying before that distressed authority could reason with him. Worse was to follow. The Directors, when the memorial ultimately reached them, sent forth a despatch which was so ambiguous and faint-hearted that Sir Peregrine Maitland, the Commander-in-Chief of Madras, resigned, after refusing to punish a European soldier who would not take part in a ceremonial guard for the salutation of a heathen deity. A Madras civilian followed his example. And here was Lord Auckland faced by the memory of a censured bishop, whose saintly life and untimely death left an uncomfortable flavour of martyrdom, and by the resignation, official but by no means temperamental, of a distinguished soldier who stood high in 'The Duke's' esteem. Fortunately for the Government discipline still remained for the Duke the cardinal virtue. He condemned Sir Peregrine's action, but showed his approval of his spirit by getting for him the governorship of the Cape. And the Directors were still faced by the question, 'How to dispose of our idolatrous commitments!'

It must indeed have been embarrassing for men exposed to the full force of the evangelical revival to hear such phrases as 'Dry nurse to Vishnu', and 'Churchwarden of Juggernaut' applied to the Company that they directed. Yet the process by which they had been made responsible for the patronage and support of heathen institutions was natural and almost inevitable. The Company in taking over the assets of those who preceded them in the rule of India had accepted also their liabilities, religious as well as secular. Its aim from the start was to create a feeling of security among its native subjects. This involved the recognition of existing and long-established rights and privileges. The Bengal regulations of 1793 guaranteed the application of the laws of the Shastras and Koran wherever they were not in conflict with peace and justice. Wellesley promised the Carnatic in 1801 not only the full enjoyment of every just and ascertained civil right, but also a free exercise of religious institutions and domestic usages of ancestors.

This guarantee involved first and foremost the continuance of all state endowments of Hindu and Mohammedan worship. And in no country, as Sir Alfred Lyall[1] has reminded us, were the popular religions more richly endowed than in India. According to Hindu ideas of sovereignty a ruler must endow his own religion liberally ; he ought, if he is liberal, to endow other local religions ; and all religions can claim his sympathy, advice, and administrative help. We succeeded rulers who had for the most part observed these principles. To the honour of India it must be said that at no time has any determined opposition been made to expenditure by the British Government on its own religious establishment or in aid of missions' medical or educational work that has avowedly a religious purpose. And India found no suggestion of apostasy in the annual allotment by a Christian Government of a sum for 'support of mosques, temples, *and other pious and beneficent purposes*'. But it was perhaps natural that the Mission world of the 'thirties should deprecate the suggestion conveyed by the phrase. It viewed too with alarm the increase in the amount of total endowment, due to the sounder administration of estates and property that had been set apart for such endowment. And it shuddered when Lord Wellesley bluntly referred to 'religious institutions of the Hindu faith maintained by the British Government'.

The Government was also committed by precedent to the patronage and protection of religious institutions and ceremonies. Civil and military officers were deputed to represent it at great festivals and the Company's troops fired deferential salutes. For the protection and comfort of pilgrims careful arrangements were made. Men of

[1] Asiatic Studies.

all religions were collected, by force if necessary, to drag the idol's car. Heber records the punishment by a British magistrate of an Indian Christian who refused to be impressed for this purpose. But there is also evidence that some refused to countenance such a clear violation of the pledge to respect religious prejudice.

Many, but for the most part innocent, were the heathen practices taken over generally from our predecessors. A military salute announced the sighting of the New Moon that ushered in Ramzan. A coconut was officially broken at the burst of the Monsoon. Brahmins were officially employed for the invocation of propitious weather. Government offices, though open on Sundays, were closed on heathen festivals. Government records were dedicated to Ganesh and Government letters were prepared with the Hindu invocation 'Sri'. Just as the Company's coinage up to 1830 retained the effigy of the no longer great Mogul, so their attitude towards their subjects' religions showed a determination to avoid all breach with the past. Relations with other countries were marked by equally comprehensive geniality. There was no flutter in the Bengal Secretariat when a draft was prepared of congratulations from the Governor-General of India to the Grand Lama of Thibet on his recent incarnation.

Lord Ellenborough throughout his term of office was haunted by the fear of arousing the Hindu world by any action capable of misinterpretation as a Christian gesture. In 1842 he conceived a heroic scheme for reassuring the Hindu mind. The Kabul mission was ordered to bring back from Ghazni the gates of the Somnath temple which had been carried off in triumph by the iconoclastic invader Mahmud many centuries before. They were to be restored to their original position as a sign of the Company's determination to protect the Hindu faith. The idea was calculated, as the Bombay Chief Secretary made bold to remark, 'to astonish the whole Christian world'. Its actual result was to provide humorists with a fertile topic and Macaulay with suitable material for a speech by which he subsequently succeeded in procuring Ellenborough's recall. Enquiry revealed that there was no proof that Somnath, no longer a place of worship, had any such gates in its temple, the site of which had become the resort of swine. The 'idol' that had been destroyed there by Mahmud was a phallic emblem of Siva worship. The neighbouring Brahmins were in 1842 Vaishnavites who showed no anxiety to recover such an emblem. As Somnath was situated in a well affected Mohammedan state the result of the restoration on the local authorities deserved consideration! Chastened but not subdued by these facts Ellenborough decided to proclaim the restoration as a national rather than a religious tribute. Ultimately the gates got no further than Agra and passed with Ellenborough's recall out of history.

To endowment, patronage, and support were added the duties of administration. The Englishman, in India anyhow, hates 'to see a job badly done'; he superintended with a relish the affairs of any temple or mosque in his administrative area for which the Company was in anyway responsible. Nothing came amiss to him and his work was thorough. Whether it was the appointment of temple staff, or regulations for dancing girls, temple fees, or pilgrims' certificates, or the collection of local dues, everything was done decently and in order, with a lavish expenditure of government paper and time. Corruption was checked and 'Moloch protected from the felony of his own servants'.

Moreover if the Company's money and its servants' time were to be spent on such work it was but reasonable that any *quid pro quo* that had been enjoyed by its predecessors should be retained by the Company and augmented, if possible, by sound administration. It was not only on the expenditure side of the estimates that temples and mosques figured. Something too was to be shown on the receipts side, in the shape of pilgrim taxes and the like. It was so easy to meet demands from the Christian world for their abolition by the reply that it would be interpreted by Islam as a concession to Hinduism. Had not even the missionaries objected to reduction of the tax as a step calculated to increase the popularity of pilgrimage!

It is improbable that anyone in India or England read into this tender dry nursing of Hindu and Mohammedan religious institutions any subordination by the Government of Christian to Hindu or Islamic cults. But it was possible to infer from it indifference to all religion. And it was certainly unfortunate that a Government which shrank timidly from any open identification with Christian propaganda should assist institutions and ceremonies that were calculated to keep the other religions of the country in a lively and flourishing condition. The Madras Comic Almanack of 1837 records the bestowal of the Order of British India on Kilpauk Chittaldroog 'for having proved that the procession of Juggernaut is eminently calculated to advance the cause of civilisation and to enlighten the minds of the Hindus in general and the lower orders in particular'. Under a benevolent Government in fact there was a boom in indigenous religions. Thackeray reminds us that the Bundelcund Banking Company throve on it.[1] 'The order from Birmingham for idols alone (made with their copper and paid in their wool) was enough to make the low church party in England cry out; and a debate on the subject took place in the House of Commons, of which the effect was to send up the shares of the B.B.C. on the London Exchange.'

[1] The Newcomes.

The polytheistic liabilities of the Company in fact were not merely being honoured. They were being considerably enlarged. The Company's servants, unable to endure the sight of inefficiency and peculation, often intervened to save a temple and became in course of time more than mother and father to the object of their attention. In 1796 Collector Place prevailed on the Fort St. George Government to take over the administration of a famous Vaishnavite shrine at Conjeeveram in south India. The reasons put forward were that the proper and regular conduct of religious ceremonies conduced to the happiness of the Company's subjects. (It was at the time impossible to get money allotted for the building of churches, and the Directors for economy were keeping chaplains' posts unfilled !) Moreover such interest on Government's part 'conciliated' the people. Place himself presented jewels to the Temple which are still on view there. And the residents fifty years later scandalised Alexander Duff by relating all that a benevolent Sircar had done for their local shrine. In 1833 the Madras Government reported that the administration of 7600 Hindu shrines was vested in the Government. 'Our connection with Hindu idolatry has grown with our greatness. Religious institutions did not receive previously the same measure of support.'

By this time it was clear to the Directors that something must be done, if not to placate evangelical critics, at least to make their attitude consistent with the policy of 'strict neutrality' which was always emphasised when Christian claims were advanced. It was in this same year, 1833, that they had opposed any increase in the episcopal establishment of India on the grounds that it was an unfair charge on 'pagan revenues'. But two Bishops were added in spite of the protest. With Daniel Wilson and Corrie using their episcopal influence and personal popularity in Calcutta and Madras, with a ruthless reformer like Bentinck at Government House, with Alexander Duff and John Wilson leading the missionaries of Bengal and Bombay, and with one of their own number, Charles Grant's son, filling the mind of the President of the Board of Control with evangelical ideas, words anyhow were necessary. Perhaps they would obviate the need for action that could only lead to trouble.

Before 1833 had closed, and with the memory of humiliating concessions enforced in the revised charter of that year fresh upon them, the Directors 'reviewed the situation' in a despatch. Toleration and civil protection of religion must on no account be converted into patronage of what is at variance with the precepts and practices of Christianity. Government's intimate connection with unhappy and debasing superstitions inspired a belief that it admitted their divine origin. It is distressing to give up what not only conciliates the people but in places yields substantial profit. Yet it is necessary to give up all internal management of temples and mosques, all revenue arising out of idolatry, and all official attendance at, or recognition of, festivals. No government officer must any longer collect fees for a temple or receive money for its management. Time must of course be allowed for adjustment. And all governments were asked for further information regarding present commitments and possible difficulties.

No one with any knowledge of government offices in India could have failed to see the opening left by this closing request for information. For the next few years the despatch produced no results, except masses of statistics and endless notes and minutes on the difficulties, many of them very real, involved by these orders. In 1837 came the petition from Madras and the Peregrine Maitland affair. The question was raised in Parliament and critics did not fail to remember that a bishop had been censured, and a commander-in-chief forced to resign, for action strictly in accordance with the general tenor of the 1833 despatch. Influential civil servants of the Company were beginning to kick. A member of the Madras board of revenue in protesting against expenditure on temple repairs stigmatised it boldly as 'a step in a direction contrary to truth'.

As a result of parliamentary pressure orders issued in 1838 for 'immediate compliance' with the instructions of 1833. The phrase was interpreted with the freedom from pedantic exactitude customary to officials faced with embarrassing orders. It took only two more years to abolish the pilgrim tax. But it was not till six years after the meeting that government officers were finally relieved of all religious duties and responsibilities, including the preservation of buildings, management of funds and appointment of temple officers. In spite of a protest from the Bombay missionary conference, which argued that no treaties contrary to the laws of God can be binding, the Government rightly refused to abolish any kind of endowment which had been recognised and taken over as a liability from their predecessors.

The gradual withdrawal of Government from management and patronage was undoubtedly responsible for some of its unpopularity in 1857. That it was merely a corollary of the doctrine of neutrality was ignored by the many who found grounds for suspicion in all the actions of Government, and not least in its nervous dread of any appearance of friendship towards Christianity. It may be true that suspicion was exacerbated by the consistent pressure brought to bear on Government by Christian missions and their supporters during the long drawn-out affair. Such pressure was perhaps impolitic; but if the Government had only asserted boldly at the outset its determination to be absolutely impartial in its application of neutrality, and if prompt action had followed such a pronouncement, there would have bee: no need for pressure nor grounds for suspicion.

The tacit recognition by the Government of cast distinctions was from time to time cited as anothe instance of weak concession to religious prejudice The charter of 1833 had confirmed and applied to al the Company's possessions the principle already formu lated by Bentinck in Bengal, that 'no disabilities ii respect of any place, office or employment should b(recognised by reason of religion, place of birth, descent or colour'. We have seen already how ineffective thi declaration was in estaolishing the claims of Indiar Christians to government service. The difficulty there was one of religion rather than caste; for Indian Christians, however low their caste prior to conversion were recognised as superior to outcastes and pariahs they were not in the same way or to the same extent a source of pollution. The total illiteracy and economic suppression of the outcastes during this period postponed effectively all question of their employment to any posts except those of the meanest and humblest description. That they were not appointed, or appointed only in very small numbers, even to such posts was due not to any deference to Hindu feeling, but to recognition of the fact that the aversion they would arouse, and the ostracism they would undergo, would prevent them from being either happy or useful in such posts. The same difficulty is felt to-day. It was felt moreover that the habits of those who had not come under Christian influence were such as to disqualify them for any work that brought them into close contact with other castes. Macaulay, during the short period of his control of education in Bengal, applied the principle of the 1833 charter in declaring all schools open to all castes. But this remained for the most part a dead letter, partly because few outcastes during this period had any desire to see their children educated, and partly because fewer still were prepared to submit themselves or their children to the persecution that would inevitably attend those who took advantage of this proclamation.

All that can be laid to the door of Government in this matter is that they refused to take any active steps to educate public opinion or to suppress the many forms of persecution that were not obviously criminal. Their failure was in a sphere where stronger and more experienced Governments of later time have failed. Nor was it possible for Christian missions, during the earlier part of the period at least, to set forth their own actions or policy as an example. It took them many years to set their own house in order. Though the earliest Protestant missionaries in the south of India, where caste feeling is most emphatic, had definitely forbidden all caste distinctions among their converts, such distinctions had slowly but steadily obtained recognition, until by the end of the eighteenth century there was little to choose in this matter between Protestant and Roman Catholic Missions, which from earliest times have recognised, and still continue in some measure to recognise, caste. Even Schwartz, though opposed to it in principle, found it necessary to deal very gently with its manifestations and checked only its most extreme and barbarous forms. When Bishop Heber visited South India in 1826 he found it impossible to induce caste Christians to assemble or take the Sacrament with pariah Christians.

Heber's tact, moderation, and comprehensive humanity led him at first to question the expediency of any frontal attack on caste. He was inclined to accept Schwartz's compromise, and to await hopefully the undermining of the evil by slow permeation of Christian principles. He saw however the need for further enquiry which ultimately revealed the division of missionaries into two almost equal camps, and the existence of a very bitter feeling among caste Christians against any drastic condemnation of caste. Heber's death left the final settlement of the matter to Bishop Wilson, whose strong and decisive campaign against all caste distinction determined for the future the policy of Protestant Missions.[1] It would be out of place to describe here the tact, firmness, and humour displayed by the bishop during the long negotiations. No one who has ever engaged in ecclesiastical controversy, particularly in the East, could fail to be impressed by his magnificent urbanity in the closing stages. Assailed by a hot-tempered and prolix champion of caste the bishop 'ignored his arguments and complimented him on his English'. Such a man deserved the triumph he won when shortly afterwards pariah and caste men knelt side by side before the altar.

But what concerns us more is the violence of the antagonism aroused by the bishop's action, and the fact that his opponents in the Indian Christian world thought it worth while to appeal to the Government. The Government indeed considered at one time the possibility of intervention. The Directors were wise enough to turn a deaf ear. The story as a whole shows the strength of caste even in a sphere that had been subjected to Christian influence; it illustrates the general conception of Government at that time as the defender *de jure* of all indigenous belief and custom; and it explains why the Government was able to make so little headway against caste and why this particular omission on their part received, comparatively, so little criticism in definitely Christian circles.

It was certainly hard on the sorely perplexed Directors that, at the very time when outside pressure was forcing them to forbid all official connection of the Company's

[1] Historically the Baptists had been the first to disallow caste.

servants with Hindu and Mohammedan religious institutions and ceremonies, their attention should repeatedly be drawn to the open support and patronage of Christian mission undertakings by influential and conspicuous officials. We have already had occasion to notice the eager and active participation of men such as the Lawrences and Edwardes in all forms of Christian propagation. What was a Government pledged conclusively to 'neutrality' to do with such champions, or with the many others who by chairmanship of committees (even by teaching in Sunday schools !) definitely suggested to the 'ex hypothesi' sensitive Indian mind that British officials really acted on the faith that they professed !

That any strong resentment or deep suspicion was engendered by such open interest in Christian work is a theory that rests on no satisfactory evidence. It seems to have originated in the nervous anxiety of those who by their shilly-shallying and restless manœuvres created in actual fact the suspicion that they foolishly ascribed to the action of their more self-confident subordinates. Periodic attempts were made to stop all open support of missions by officials. Many years elapsed before a distinction was systematically made between what was done by a supporter in his official and in his private capacity. While distracted secretaries were fumbling after this distinction, attempts were made to distinguish 'open and tactless' from 'discreet and tactful' support. The Indian public in consequence was misled into confusing the straightforward and honest Christian undertakings of men acting in a private not official capacity with the furtive intrigues of influential officials. Undertakings of the former type have never excited alarm in India. Suspicion of the latter has been ever a fruitful cause of riot and rebellion.

Such misunderstanding could not but arise from

orders forbidding the Company's chaplains to use mission chapels for their services, lest their connection with mission work should be suspected, or from a carefully worded despatch emphasising the danger of all religious discussion or enquiry in government schools and colleges. In 1847 the Directors 'reminded' government servants that they must abstain from interference with the religions of the natives of India and vaguely 'drew attention' to acts of indiscretion without giving particulars. The Government of India was puzzled and alarmed by the gloom of this warning. 'Did it', they asked, with an unusual flash of inspiration, 'cover the private acts of officials?' This was too much for tired and harassed Directors. 'The application of the rule', they replied gravely, 'should be governed by the principles on which it is founded!'

Never had words been used more carefully to conceal meaning. But by this time the Indian Government was beginning to enjoy the game. Back went the shuttlecock. 'Could civil and military officers in their private capacity promote mission work, or could they not?' Once again the Directors rallied for a supreme effort. 'Yes, private funds may be contributed to missions. But there must be no manifestation of a disposition calculated to excite uneasiness or alarm.' Official jargon is always difficult to translate. But what the Directors had apparently at the back of their distraught minds was a desiro to make Christian-spirited officials in India responsible beforehand for any suspicions that the vague suggestions of Leadenhall Street might arouse in India. Similar bleatings followed riots in Bombay caused by the conversion of some Parsees in 1879. 'Civil servants must be careful in the use of their legitimate influence lest their efforts should be misrepresented'. In spite of Dalhousie's efforts in the direction of a bolder and more resolute 'declaration of rights' the situation remained obscure, and consequently to the native mind confusing and ominous, up to the time of the Mutiny.

The case of Prabhu Din Naick may illustrate and close this tale of nervous indecision. In 1819 a sepoy of this name in a Brahmin regiment of the Bengal army was converted and baptised by a Company chaplain called Fisher. This 'singular and unprecedented' event roused the commanding officer to complain to his superior officer. His consent had not been obtained (presumably by the Chaplain not the Holy Spirit) and recruiting was likely to be affected. In due course the file reached the Governor-General. The erring Naick was suspended and a full enquiry ordered.

The chaplain reported that he had not primarily been responsible for the lapse from ancestral faith. The downward path had been begun nine years before in Mauritius. But he had answered enquiries made in person at his house by the sepoy and had always allowed sepoys to attend his services if they wished to do so. His baptism had followed his earnest entreaties in the face of bribes and threats from his companions. Since his conversion there had been no complaints on the score of slackness in military duties. No disturbance had taken place and persecution by his comrades had ceased. The court of enquiry added that no chaplain or missionary had ever entered the military lines. Fisher's action and general attitude were supported by Bishop Middleton, a man not likely to spare evangelical indiscretion when detected; Bishop Heber, who saw the papers, later acquitted Fisher of all blame. The Government, however, refused to reinstate the sepoy in his regiment. He was retired on full pay and refused with proper pride an offer subsequently made to admit him to another regiment. A general impression was created throughout the Bengal army that the Government was not prepared openly to tolerate Christianity. What the Government was really aiming at only God knew. But the army had its suspicions. About the same time the commanding officer of the 14th Foot reported that the Christian sepoys in his regiment were far the best.

CHAPTER XII

MISSION INFLUENCE ON EDUCATION. DUFF AND WILSON

Educational protagonists—Bentinck, Dalhousie, Duff, Wilson—early educational efforts—doubts regarding grants to mission schools—Anglicists and Orientalists in 1835—mission share in Bentinck's decision—Macaulay's faith in secular education—and its first fruits—the 'Home of Learning'—David Hare and De Rozio—oriental reaction—final triumph of the West—need for religious education recognised—mission co-operation secured by Wood's despatch, 1854—approval of Ram Mohun Roy and Hindu reformers—absence of orthodox opposition.

DURING the period now under review the educational policy of the British Government in India was formulated and ultimately embodied in a system which has continued unchanged in its main features up to the present day. In the shaping of this policy, and in the elaboration of the system, the British Government was brought into close and eventually most friendly touch with Christian agencies. In no sphere of Indian administration have these agencies been able to demonstrate more effectively their usefulness to the State or their capacity for co-operation. There has in fact been a tendency to identify the interests of Government and Christian missions; and it will be necessary to discuss later whether the missions have profited as much as the Government from this identification.

Three principles were clearly established during this period. The first defines and limits the educational responsibilities of the British Government. Accepting the task of advancing by education the moral and material progress of the Indian peoples, the Government finally dissociated itself from any form, however vague and unsectarian, of religious teaching. The remaining two principles explain the inclusion of Christian mission institutions within the Government system. The missions definitely included education of all kinds and grades, among their instruments for the evangelisation of India. And the Government was led gradually to recognise the inevitable need for the co-operation of missions, and the possibility of ensuring this co-operation by financial assistance, without departure from the previously established principle of religious neutrality.

With these principles the names of the boldest Governors-General, Bentinck and Dalhousie, and of the great Scotch missionaries, Alexander Duff and John Wilson, are closely associated. Dalhousie alone accepted everything that the three principles implied. Bentinck, without the experience that guided Dalhousie, doubted the wisdom of Government grants to mission institutions. Duff and Wilson throughout, though with gradually waning emphasis, deprecated the dissociation of the Government from all forms of religious instruction. It was Duff who slowly but surely convinced the Mission world by the success of his experiments and the persistent fearlessness of his speeches and pamphlets, that success depended on the enlightenment of India by Christian secondary schools and colleges. It was not easy to convince a home committee scared, in the troubled 'thirties, by such boldness 'in these days of agitation, turmoil, revolutionary tendencies and irregularities of every description'. Duff's task, as he was ready to admit, was facilitated by Bentinck's bold determination that the energy of the British in India should be concentrated on securing for those committed to their care the choicest gifts of western civilisation. All alike believed that they were preparing a mine which would ultimately overthrow all religious and social obstacles to the progress of India.

It would be grossly unfair to Schwartz and Carey to suggest that educational work had been entirely neglected by Christian missions before Duff began his Indian work in 1830. In south India Schwartz had spread a network of vernacular schools. English education had been attempted in Tanjore, though it hardly survived the death of Schwartz. The London Mission had a system of vernacular schools in Bengal by the time that the Baptist Marshman, with the help of Ram Mohun Roy and Dwarkanath Tagore inaugurated their Bengali schools in 1816. In 1818 the great Baptist mission college in Serhampore had been opened. Here Carey's genius conceived the idea of a 'Christian Benares' where Christian scholars would be steeped in oriental and western learning, and Indians of all castes would have access to the best that east and west could jointly provide. Without any assistance from public funds, from the literary earnings and press profits of the devoted band of missionaries, a stately building rose in which two hundred students, including eleven Brahmins and three Mohammedans, were shortly enrolled. Thirty pundits from all parts of India attended the first examination of the college. The King of Denmark gave the land and granted in 1827 a royal charter which authorised the college to grant degrees in all faculties. Serhampore is now under the British flag. But the curious investigator is still reminded of the debt that Christian missions and Indian education owe to this gallant little Danish settlement by the unique privilege retained by the college, as a relic of its Danish charter, of conferring degrees in Christian theology.

The Anglican faith could hardly emulate the Baptists' zeal. In 1820 the foundation of Bishop's College, Calcutta, recorded the educational first-fruits of the episcopal establishment granted in 1813. In seven years a cautious bishop had satisfied himself and the

Government that India would not resent this reminder of Christian intrusion.

But the foundation of Serhampore College exhausted the first fine careless rapture of the Baptists. The opposition of their home committee to ambitious educational schemes continued. And the evangelical supporters of Anglican missions were far more interested in the dissemination of the Bible and baptismal statistics than in any measures for the general enlightenment of India. Duff's fiery personality, and the work by which personally he sustained the cause that he had at heart, did what even Schwartz and Carey could not in this particular field have done. The Scotch belief in education triumphed. All Calcutta, official, mercantile and military, Europeans and Indians, used to attend his periodical examinations of the students of his College, and marvel at the stream of 'useful information', scientific, historical, literary, and theological that he pumped out of his Bengali pupils. It was the age of Children's Guides to Knowledge. And Duff was Bengal's guide.

But many years were to pass before the official world was prepared to do more than politely admire such work. The policy of financial aid to mission schools was not officially approved till Wood's despatch of 1854. Characteristically the governments in various provinces gave grants to individual schools here and there from 1813 onwards, regardless of the possibility of misinterpretation of their motives. Lord Hardinge visited Serhampore and inspected mission schools. Lord Hastings became a patron of the college and subscribed to its funds. In 1835 Lord Clive asked the Scotch Mission to continue to give religious instruction in the Poona schools that had been taken over by the Government. But no less characteristic were the many instances of refusal of grants or even recognition and patronage. Amherst refused a grant to Bishops College, and Bentinck was bold enough to reject an application from Duff's institution. A similar application from a school intended for Calcutta ladies was dismissed in spite of a strong recommendation from the Governor-General's Council. Thirty years later only Dalhousie's resolute persistence won for the Bethune girls' school in Calcutta the privilege of having on its council a prominent member of Council and of enjoying the official recognition of the Government. It was one thing to aim at educating male India for administrative and professional work, and quite another thing to invade the privacy of the Indian home by tampering with the ideas and outlook of Indian women.

The old fear was in fact constantly reasserting itself. Growing interest in Christian activities for the welfare of India was periodically checked by the thought that misinterpretation of such interest might lead to popular tumult. But gradually and persistently Duff and Wilson were producing results that justified Dalhousie's bold declaration of 1854. 'We carry the principle of neutrality too far. Even from the political point of view we err in ignoring so completely as we do the agency of ministers of our own true faith in extending education among the people.' Consistently with this declaration he was encouraging provincial governments to aid liberally mission education a few years before Wood's despatch of 1854 set the seal of the Board of Control's approval on his policy.

The cause of mission education was in fact substantially advanced by the controversy that preceded Bentinck's famous declaration of 1835 in favour of western education and by the substance of that declaration. Though the question of religion was directly discussed in none of the acrimonious minutes that passed between Orientalists and Anglicists, the superior eloquence and ruthlessness of the Anglicists undoubtedly created a strong prejudice against Hinduism and Islam of which Duff and Wilson were not slow to take advantage. Macaulay refused to allow for one moment the claims of the indigenous religions to be admitted in favour of oriental studies. Even the Directors, forgetting for the moment their passionate fear of arousing Indian hostility, ventured to find fault with those who had advocated the study of the Indian classics. They had suggested 'any learning that is useful; but poetry is not useful and we suspect that there is little in Hindu or Mohammedan literature that is'. From such a declaration it was only a short step to the opinion expressed by the Council of Instruction that 'only the missions can educate the lower classes'.

The final defeat of the Orientalists, by a declaration that Prinsep,[1] Oriental protagonist, compared to the burning of the library at Alexandria, emphasised the utilitarian and moral aspects of the Government's educational policy. There may be interpreters of the Sermon on the Mount who question its essential association with utilitarian aims or the importing of useful information. But Duff was not one of these and he made it his purpose to convince the Government that in both these aims they had the support of missions. On the government side there were many who believed that the missions could count ultimately on corresponding support from Government.

Macaulay and Trevelyan[2] alike believed that large and continuous doses of western knowledge would not only purge India of Hindu and Islamic religions, but also build up a new India with an essentially Christian

[1] H.T.P. Member of Bengal Council and subsequently Director of East India Co.

[2] C. E. T., brother-in-law of Macaulay; civil servant; Governor of Madras; took active part in shaping Indian educational policy.

constitution. When Macaulay prophesied that in forty years' time there would not be an idolator left in Bengal his joy and hopefulness were no doubt Christian ; but it was to 'Wisdom while you Wait' rather than the Bible that he looked for the fulfilment of his hope.

It was David Hare, watchmaker and positivist, who by his educational work first caused these official optimists to wonder whether the effect of undiluted western information would be what they had at first so confidently predicted. Hare was a philanthropist who took an active interest in every movement that affected the moral and intellectual improvement of Bengal, except that which was directed to the propagation of Christianity. The five thousand Hindus who followed his body to the grave rightly saw in him a man who had dedicated his life to Indian progress. After earning for himself in the first sixteen years of the nineteenth century a competence that would have enabled him to live thenceforth at ease in England he stayed in India, as his Calcutta statue tells us, 'to promote the welfare of the land of his adoption'. Amongst other things he was the first to draw the attention of Government to the treatment of indentured Indian coolies in Mauritius.

To David Hare the founders of the Vidyalaya turned in 1817. This 'Home of Learning', which grew into the Hindu College, and ultimately into the Government Presidency College of Calcutta, represented a determination on the part of an influential band of Hindu reformers in Calcutta to secure for the Hindu world the benefits of western education without the addition of Christian teaching.

The co-operation of the great reformer, Ram Mohun Roy, friend and counsellor of Bentinck, involved an equally antagonistic attitude towards Hindu orthodoxy. In Hare they found a leader after their own heart. For many years he inspired and directed this educational venture. Its success was partially at least responsible for Bentinck's belief that India really desired and was capable of using western education. For us its interest consists mainly in the fact that it was the first experiment in the direction of a purely and avowedly secular education that India had seen.

Its influence was soon felt. The principal, De Rozio, presents himself as 'a Free-thinker possessed of affable manners'. His chief battle-cry was 'down with Hinduism'. He founded a paper called *The Parthenon*, one of his theories apparently being that a religion after it had ceased to function became harmless and ornamental. His enemies, who were numerous, accused him among other things of having advocated incest through the medium of his paper. Among his early disciples was Radha Nath Sickdar. 'His hobby was beef and he maintained that beef eaters were never bullied.' Another stalwart beef eater studied Paley's evidences as the basis of a series of articles against the Christian religion.

It is not surprising to find the committee of public instruction reporting before long that 'the moral effect of this institution has been remarkable. Impatience of the instructions of Hinduism and disregard of its ceremonies are openly avowed by some and secretly entertained by others'. Before long even the most secularist of the managers feared that De Rozio was really going too far in his undermining of all religious influence. His substitution of extracts from Pope's Iliad for the usual Brahmin prayers was perhaps pardonable. But what was to be said of a dinner party of students which ended with the hurling of beef fragments into the courtyard of a neighbouring Brahmin!

De Rozio was dismissed and an order promulgated against the use of books subversive of morality and decency. The students to mark their resentment left the college in a body and resorted to Duff's College.

Even Christian instruction was better than the drab enforcement of respect for Hindu prejudice.

By this time Hare's connection with the college had ceased. That he had a sense of humour is suggested by his Hindu biographer who reports with surprise that, when greeted by a grateful student with the words, 'Thou art the mother that has suckled us', he 'shrugged his head and showed a smile on his face'. It was perhaps in order to avoid such embarrassing compliments that he accepted a judgeship in the Court of Small Causes. Up to the end of his life he was to be found in his blue coat and old-fashioned gaiters engaged in acts of quiet and unobtrusive friendliness to all Hindus.

But if Hare had gone, his work survived, as did also the more aggressive spirit of De Rozio. Among the College textbooks we find Hume's *Essays on Restoration Comedy* and Tom Paine's *Age of Reason*. Its debating society accepts unanimously an ample resolution covering all the Rights of Man.

This 'Home of Learning' from an early stage, and up to the time of its passing under Government control, was in receipt of financial help from the Government. But what perplexed even the most optimistic of its official supporters was the obvious fact that its students at the close of its secularist regime were far more interested in the rights than in the duties of man. Intoxicated with the heady wine of western learning they were playfully inclined to tilt at everything, and particularly their own religion and society. But they had no designs or foundations for any substitute. A few, and notably the liberal-minded Krishna Mohan Bannerji, joined Duff's class of 'enquirers' and ultimately after a long pilgrim's progress became his most zealous disciples. But more were permanently content with the licence that they mistook for liberty and regarded the power that western knowledge gave them merely as a means of shaking off social connections that had become irksome. If western education meant only or primarily the flouting of caste rules its doom was certain.

There was of course an inevitable reaction in favour of oriental learning, supported, as Duff thought, by Lord Auckland, whose well-meant efforts to draw India's attention to the educational possibilities of her own classics was stigmatised as 'an official system of education which jealously excludes all true religion'. But even without such attacks Auckland's plans, though justifiable, were doomed to failure. India was not at this stage going to forego the delights of western knowledge which she had just begun to enjoy. Government offices were clamouring for more and more English-knowing clerks. Brahmins in the newly founded medical classes were making up their minds to dissect corpses. The work must go on. But what was to be the social and moral equivalent of caste? And how was western education to be converted from an excuse for license into an instrument for the right and sober use of liberty?

It was fortunate for India that just when this question called for an answer, the impossibility of adequate provision being made by Government for all who desired western education was also becoming manifest. Both problems were solved by the Education Despatch of 1854, which followed the parliamentary enquiry and renewal of the Company's charter in 1853. This despatch owed much to the evidence given by Duff, Marshman and other missionaries before the parliamentary committee. Its ultimate form was due to the wise and farseeing mind of Charles Wood. The inauguration of the complete system of education which it prescribed was facilitated by the eager support of Dalhousie who had already anticipated some of its principles.

The Despatch provided amongst other things for a comprehensive system of grants in aid to all institutions under private management that submitted themselves to inspection and fulfilled the conditions of sound education prescribed by Government. Though all reference to the work of Christian missions was carefully excluded from this portion of the Despatch, there could be no doubt that it was their co-operation that the Board of Control hoped chiefly to invite by this offer of financial assistance. There were in fact comparatively few institutions under any other form of private management at the time. Charles Wood reaffirmed emphatically the intention of the British Government to raise by education the moral standard of India and made it quite clear that 'the noble exertions of mission societies to guide the natives of India in the way of religious truth' were duly appreciated by all who emphasised this moral aim. It was clearly satisfactory that the agency which alone could hope to supplement the educational efforts of the Government was also in a position to supply the religious foundation of moral instructions which official institutions lacked. That it was possible for a 'neutral' Government to give a grant to all institutions alike, irrespective of their religious aims and with reference solely to their secular work, was established finally and categorically. It is true that the nervous and fussy Lord Ellenborough, who, by a change of government, assumed charge of the Board of Control soon after the despatch issued, refused to give it this interpretation and rejected a proposal to aid C.M.S. work among the primitive tribes of Bengal on the grounds that it was a violation of 'neutrality'. But in spite of his protests Wood's policy was maintained locally. Figures collected in 1859 showed that mission institutions in the Madras Presidency were receiving five times as much grant as all other private institutions put together. Almost all the aided secondary schools were under mission control. The provincial Government was satisfied that this generous help to missions had roused no resentment at all. It was significant that the province which had done most for missions was also the province which had remained completely quiet in the year of Mutiny.

Undoubtedly the cordial relations that had been established between Duff and the earnest and influential band of non-Christian Hindu reformers had helped to dispel the apprehensions of Government.

Ram Mohun Roy, son of an agent of Surajud Dowlah, after renouncing idolatry at the age of sixteen, forsook the study of Persian and Sanskrit, and through the devious routes of Horace and Buddhist writers drew near to the English as the only possible agents of amelioration in India. On leaving his post of Collector's Diwan at the age of fifty he devoted himself to the study of the Bible in Hebrew and Greek and came to regard the precepts of Jesus as the only possible guide to peace and happiness. His attitude towards Brahminism was substantially that of Erasmus towards the practices of Rome. It is possible that he might have professed Christianity but for the over-zeal of some strict Baptists who condemned him as a 'legalist'. He died in 1834, a Unitarian at heart, but professing Hinduism without conscientious scruples in order to secure his property for his heirs.

It did not take Ram Mohun Roy long to find out that Duff's College was likely to do far more for the regeneration of India than Hare's 'Home of Learning . From the very start he was active in gaining the support of his Hindu friends for Duff. Bible instruction was clearly unequalled for morals. The Lord's Prayer was the best in the world. At the opening of the college he joined in this prayer and persuaded the Brahmin students to open for the first time and read the Bible which Duff had resolutely prescribed as the first textbook.

It is significant that no oriental college was opened

during this whole period as a protest against Duff's activities. We hear only of a Bombay petition against all mission schools following the conversion of some Parsees in the 'thirties, and of the formation of a Hindu anti-mission society and establishment by Jesuits and an Irish adventurer of a free anti-Protestant College in the 'forties. In fact, such opposition as Duff aroused was on western or agnostic lines and dissociated entirely from oriental orthodoxy. As such it was rightly disregarded by the Government.

CHAPTER XIII
FURTHER EDUCATIONAL PROBLEMS

Mission attitude towards oriental studies—its justification and weakness—Bible teaching in government schools—firm refusal by Government—confidence in pioneer work of secular education—exclusion of all references to religion—final settlement in Wood's despatch—no Bible teaching—but irksome restrictions removed—acquiescence of missions—faulty prognostications.

It was not only a definite and honourable place in the educational system that was won by Christian missions during this period. They also established gradually their claim to be consulted in the framing and execution of important educational measures. The part played by Duff in the discussion that preceded the decisions of 1835 and 1854 has already been noted. Before the close of the period missions were represented on most educational committees ; in the elaboration of the first Indian universities, on lines laid down in the 1854 despatch, Duff and Wilson played an influential part ; and they filled important and onerous posts in the earliest stages of Calcutta and Bombay universities. Like their predecessors, Schwartz and Carey, they had shown in fact that a good Christian is endowed with judgment and discerning tact that enhance his value in Councils of State. Their voice was often heard on subjects not directly connected with education or religion. Duff in particular had much to do with the removal of certain evils in the land tenure system of Bengal which caused popular discontent. Wilson was a constant and trustworthy referee in all questions of indigenous customs, literature, traditions and religion.

It was the missionaries no less than the Hindu reform party who kept persistently before the Government, in the years that followed the impetuous regime of Bentinck, Trevelyan, and Macaulay, the supreme importance of education. And it was the same combination of interests that sternly opposed all attempts to find a place in the curriculum for oriental culture and literature. 'In undertaking to teach mere Hindu or Mohammedan literature you bound yourselves to teach a great deal of what was frivolous, not a little of what was mischievous, and a small remainder indeed in which utility was in any way concerned.' This rebuke from the Directors in 1824 was endorsed by Duff and Wilson. It was unfortunate but perhaps inevitable that men whose attention was concentrated on the darker side of Hindu and Islamic society, and who saw in Christian teaching the only remedy for India's woes, should reject the oriental classics as wholly unsuitable for youthful consumption. They were not, like Macaulay, wholly ignorant of the literary excellence of oriental literature; nor did they deny that there was much to be found in it of moral and spiritual value. Wilson in particular was a distinguished and enthusiastic Orientalist. And Duff strongly supported the patronage by Government of oriental research and scholarship. But such work could play no part in the moral uplifting of the nation. The foundations of Indian literature were essentially false and insecure. It could never form an integral part in any scheme of natural character building.

We may rightly deplore an attitude that postponed indefinitely the methodical study of indigenous culture and cut off India from a just appreciation of the strength and weakness of all that underlay its social and religious systems. But if we remember the appalling evils that were justly associated with this culture when our education courses were being devised, and the sturdy part played by the opponents of this culture in the removal of these evils, we shall not find it hard to excuse their excess of zeal.

We may criticise the rhetorical exuberance of Duff's most famous speech in Exeter Hall. But no one who has studied his life and work can question the sincerity of his peroration or deny his ability to quote chapter and verse for his denunciation. Condemning those who wrote sentimentally of India and its

> Fields of paradise and bowers
> Entwining amaranthine flowers

he passed on to depict what he had found there ; 'above, the spiritual gloom of a gathering tempest, relieved only by the lightning glance of the Almighty's indignation—around a moral wilderness where all light dies and only death lives—and underneath one vast catacomb of immortal souls perishing for lack of knowledge'. To the culture of a land that had thus impressed its woes upon him he could not, if he would, pay educational homage.

In another sphere the advice tendered by Christian bodies was less effective. It was at one time the clear and unanimous opinion of these agencies that Christian teaching of some kind should be given in the schools and colleges maintained by the British Government. This was also the opinion of the Lawrences and Edwardes and many other stalwart Christians in the official world whose work and character has already been examined. As to the nature and extent of this teaching there was great variety of opinion. Nor was there agreement as to whether attendance at such instruction should be compulsory or not. But many agents of the Government, and practically all the agents of Christian missions, held that the gift of western civilisation, divorced from all knowledge of its religious foundations, was educationally unsound and morally dangerous. Reference to the Government's pledge of 'religious neutrality' was met by a refusal to admit that such neutrality involved the deliberate exclusion of a vital and integral part of 'western education' from courses that professed to make such education their aim. It was argued that instruction in the principles and history of Christianity, and exposition of its bearing on the history of civilisation, was possible without any suspicion of 'proselytising'. The exclusion of such subjects suggested inevitably to the Indian mind that they were regarded by the Government as unimportant.

To such arguments the government as a whole, despite the views of some of its highest officers, showed at no time any intention of capitulating. Their wisdom and the results of their decision on Indian history will be discussed separately and later. Those who realise the inevitable limitations of government schools and colleges, and the difficulties under which official teachers labour, find it hard to believe that the acceptance of missionary advice would have promoted substantially the advance of Christianity or altered the Indian attitude towards western civilisation. The solution of the problem, which was far more vital and far-reaching than the authorities realised, lay in the gradual withdrawal of the Government from the direct control and management of a higher education which was necessarily cribbed, cabined, and confined by their well-meant efforts, and in the evolution of a system of Christian education free from all the implications of a 'neutral' system. We are concerned here rather with the motives of the Government and the modes of their reaction to Christian pressure.

That Bentinck, Macaulay, and Trevelyan expected the Christianisation of India as a result of a purely secular western education has already been explained.

This view was held by a few thoughtful Christians in India and England even in later years. Canon Mozley,[1] discussing the prospects of Christianity in the 'fifties, warmly supported the ' neutral ' attitude of the Government and argued that their so-called ' godless ' education left the Indian mind purged and desiring to be filled. ' Deism ', he wrote, referring to the negative effects of such education, ' is not a possible resting-place '. He believed firmly what several witnesses before the Parliamentary committee of 1853 had affirmed, that government schools were doing pioneer work for Christianity. The students of such schools, he understood, were as distinguished for character and strength of mind as the product of mission schools and provided ultimately as many converts to Christianity.

An obvious retort to this line of argument was that, if the Government really believed that the system of education was, as they stated to their Christian critics, a valuable preparation for Christianity and a necessary stage in evangelisation, they were acting dishonestly in assuring the Indian world that it was consistent with the strictest neutrality.[2] What they were really engaged in was the undermining of a society and culture which could, under the terms of their constantly affirmed neutrality, claim their protection and respect. If they did not think that they were paving the way for Christian work they were disregarding the real interests of India in destroying the foundations of society without any thought for providing a social and moral equivalent. That the Government felt scruples on this point was clear from their readiness to accept the educational co-operation of missions and from their uneasiness at the recklessness and licence engendered by the ' Home of Learning ' in its early stages.

[1] In *Essays in History and Theology*.

[2] The dilemma is well put by Maclear in *Christian Statesmen and our Indian Empire*.

What really influenced the Government, and still more the Directors at home, was their responsibility for the maintenance of law and order in India, and their dread of endangering imperial interests or the prosperity of the country by popular discontent or suspicion. What they failed to see was the importance of removing all suspicion by a bold and resolute policy. That Christian interests would have been advanced by the introduction of Bible teaching in Government schools may well be doubted. But it is certain that the meticulous exclusion from the school curriculum of everything that could possibly be connected with the professed faith of the supreme authorities in India merely puzzled the Indian mind and did not in any way inspire confidence. Minds naturally subtle and suspicious argued that a Government which ostentatiously ignored in education a faith that they professed was false either to its own profession or to its alien subjects. Insincerity was a quality which experience had taught India to expect from her rulers. But it was not a quality which had ever strengthened a dynasty or won for it affection and respect.

This official nervousness, so fatal to all rulers of oriental races, betrayed itself in the regulations that, up to 1854, excluded the Bible even from the libraries of Government institutions, and forbade official teachers to explain any reference to religion in English literature or history, or to answer, in or out of school, any questions from students on religious topics.[1] In Jane Taylor's poems, which were introduced as a moral tonic, editorial changes respected the religious susceptibility of non-Christian readers. For 'Christian' where it occurred 'soldier' was substituted. And though Solomon was free from all Christian associations, it was thought wiser to substitute, with consequential changes, the phrase

[1] In 1849 a convert to Christianity was dismissed from the Government College in Calcutta.

'wise man' for his actual name. The story of the Hebrew race was found to be historically as dangerous and untouchable a subject as the history of Christianity. Meanwhile stories from Hindu and Mohammedan religions were, despite Duff's protests, freely admitted into the vernacular reading books. When the Madras Government proposed to include the Bible, not indeed in a school curriculum, but in the list of textbooks allowed for the examinations of candidates for public service, they were reminded by the Directors that it was 'neither expedient nor prudent to introduce any branch of study which can in any way interfere with the religious feelings and opinions of the people'. Yet Macaulay had calculated with confidence that western science would in forty years remove all traces of idolatry![1]

The Despatch of 1854 removed some of the more tiresome and ignominious restrictions. The Bible was admitted to libraries and the teacher's activities outside his classroom were no longer confined. But the exclusion of all references to Christianity in Government school courses was emphatically endorsed. And the universities, which the despatch brought into being, were to admit in their examinations for degrees no subjects connected with religious belief. To the philosophy student Butler's *Analogy* must be anathema. The professors of Sanskrit and Persian must treat these languages as if they had never been employed on religious themes.

Such was the perplexing and ambiguous world in which mission education secured a footing in 1854. To Duff and Wilson it seemed at the time a satisfactory compromise. With a fair field and no favour, adequate grants in aid and no restriction on religious instructions, Christian education would surely flourish and make good

[1] See Trevelyan, *Life and Letters of Lord Macaulay*.

the defects of the Government schools. They would perhaps have been less confident if they had foreseen the reluctance of Government to withdraw from direct participation in higher education, and the rapid growth in the number of schools and colleges ready to take advantage of the grant in aid system, but uninspired by religious motives. Lord Ellenborough was no friend to mission work in India and it was hardly to be expected that his advice would commend itself to missionaries. But there was more wisdom in his words of warning than was generally recognised when he suggested in a discussion arising out of the claims of Christian work on government support, that 'the missionary left to himself may obtain some though probably no great measure of success. Helped by Government he loses his chances and impedes the measures of Government'. What neither he nor his opponents understood was that it was not state support but identification with state machinery that might ultimately embarrass the mission cause.

CHAPTER XIV
THE MUTINY IN ITS RELIGIOUS ASPECT

Speculation on causes of Mutiny—religious apprehension one of the causes—Christian aims and methods not responsible—regions of greatest mission activity unmoved—not a 'holy war'—but genuine fear of religious interference—due to mischief makers—secular education—and misunderstanding of official oscillation—Indian respect for frank and genuine devotion—and fear of disintegrating forces—the Queen's proclamation of 1858—final acknowledgment of Christian basis—from 'neutrality' to tolerance—ready response in India—the fruits of the Mutiny in India.

When the causes of the Indian Mutiny were investigated there were not wanting those who attributed the disaster primarily to popular resentment caused by the Government's patronage and support of Christian mission work on its educational and philanthropic side, by its legislation on Christian principles against social evils, such as infanticide, suttee, and converts' loss of civil rights, and by the open profession of Christianity and support of proselytising agencies by many of its individual officers. Nor was this opinion confined to the antagonists of mission work in India. To John Lawrence and Outram the events of 1857 presented themselves as the inevitable protest of pagan barbarism against Christian civilisation. Like Lord Ellenborough they attributed the Mutiny to mission influence. But unlike the Lord of Doubting Castle, Mr. Valiant and Mr. Greatheart were convinced that they had seen the final agony of defeated Moloch.

Opposed to the Ellenborough school, though not wholly to the views of Lawrence and Outram, were those who followed Duff in finding the cause of the catastrophe in the nervous apprehension of the British Government, its dread of emphasising its true faith and occasional appearance of repudiating it, and its pandering to heathen prejudice. The penalty had been paid for the sacrifice of Christianity on the altar of worldly expediency.

We may leave out of account the various causes of discontent, whether real or imaginary, that had no connection, direct or otherwise, with religion. Undoubtedly a fear that the religions of the country, and social usage based thereon, were being attacked was, as stated by Lord Canning in his report and by Disraeli in the House of Commons, among the causes of the revolt. To what extent had the Government, by its occasional support or occasional repudiation of definitely Christian aims, been responsible for this fear?

The more plausible view, that its Christian tendencies had stirred Hindu and Islamic orthodoxy to revolt, cannot survive a reference to facts. It was not urged by any of the provincial Governments. Only one Government in fact devoted any serious consideration to it; not even this Government suggested the possibility of any change of policy in deference to such a view. The official view generally was the same as that of the Madras Government on the Vellore mutiny of 1806. Those who for other reasons wished to stir up discontent had been able to persuade an uneducated population that religion was in danger. There was no definite action or formulated policy of the British Government that could possibly be misconstrued into an attack on religion without special pleading on the part of ill-disposed persons. Except in regions where such malice had been at work there were no traces of religious excitement due to Christian legislation or administrative action.

More particularly was it noticeable that most of the trouble had occurred in Agra and Oudh, where mission work had made least progress, and in the Bengal army where caste prejudice and religious scruples had been most carefully safeguarded, where native Christians had been rigorously discouraged and attempts at conversion forbidden. In the Punjab, where officials had been singularly bold in their support of missions, there had been no widespread uprising. Mission operations in the most orthodox parts continued with the approval of the authorities throughout the mutiny. In Madras Presidency, the stronghold of Hindu orthodoxy, where Mission work had made most progress, and where Government aid to mission educational work had attracted general attention, quiet had reigned supreme. Even W. D. Arnold, who, as director of public instruction in the Punjab, had been meticulous in his regard for indigenous religions, was unable to record any popular dissatisfaction due to the financial support of mission schools.

It is true that many Indian Christians perished, not a few heroically, as martyrs for their faith. But for the most part they were singled out for their loyalty to the British rather than to their religion. The Mohammedan rebels offered sometimes the alternative of recantation. But it is characteristic of this community to convert any war or uprising in which they were engaged in to a Jehad or holy war. That they regarded thus the Mutiny when once it had started is no proof that it arose from hatred or fear of the infidel. Out of four hundred missionaries in India thirty-seven perished. But there is no evidence that their fate, or the destruction of their churches or schools, was distinguished in motive or origin from the treatment of their civilian and military fellow-sufferers.

Moreover the reaffirmation after the Mutiny of the Government's Christian faith, and the absence of any change in its attitude towards Christian work, if the view under discussion were correct, would have caused in subsequent years frequent recurrence of such trouble. But post-mutiny history records few if any uprisings similar to several that occurred between the Vellore trouble of 1806 and 1857, and no discontent as pervasive or intense as that which found vent in the latter year. The most bitter opponents of our rule in India have never found any support for an attempt to question our religious impartiality, and have rarely if ever made such an attempt.

How then are we to account for the widespread fear of interference with religion and society that had been generally admitted as one of the causes of discontent? Even if it be granted that a superstitious and illiterate population can be led by clever and unscrupulous mischief makers with real or imaginary grievances, we must look for other factors as well if we are to account satisfactorily for so forcible and extensive a conviction. One obvious reason will be suggested by the scandal caused in Calcutta by the extravagance of the Hindu college students in its earlier days and the licence that followed De Rozio's excursions in western civilisation. It was not the Christian aims of Government but the apparent lack of any religious aim that frightened many observers of its educational efforts. To many its schools must have seemed to be explosive and disintegrating forces, likely to result in the dissolution of society and of everything that brought a feeling of stable security to the conservative home-loving Hindu. Equally frightening were the railways and telegraphs and all the symbols and instruments of an alien civilisation, that seemed likely to absorb all that was pleasantly familiar without making any contribution to the spiritual and religious values of the Hindu home.

It was quite certain that caste feeling and religious scruples hampered the Feringhi in his commercial and materialistic designs. How was he to find customers or sellers for his English boots and shoes so long as leather was offensive to the orthodox Hindu? And it seemed likely also that he found the sepoy less useful for garrison service or imperialistic aggression because of the restrictions imposed by orthodoxy. Of what use were men who resented being sent across the seas to fight, or who rejected the meat diet that would fit them for strenuous work in cold climates? What, from the Feringhi's point of view, could be more natural or in fact inevitable than that he should try, for selfish reasons and by trickery or force, to mould the customs of India to his liking? The open use of force was indeed not to be feared. For the mistakes of Aurungzeb and the triumph of Sivaji had not been forgotten. But guile could accomplish what open compulsion might fail to do. Hence this much advertised pledge of neutrality. Hence these schools when the young were taught to despise the manners and customs of their fathers; these railways where pariah and Brahmin were herded together.

It was not Christian influence, nor indeed the intrusion of any new religion, that caused a panic, but the selfish and destructive motives attributed, partly in cunning and partly *bona fide*, by priests and potentates to government action which seemed to threaten their interests. 'Let Government act openly as a Christian government,' wrote a Hindu official in the height of the tumult. 'Let it pay missionaries and distribute Bibles. But let it not use its strength or force to interfere with caste'.

If the Government had resolutely declared its belief that the religion which it represented provided the only complete remedy for India's troubles, if it had pointed out at the same time that the spirit of Christ relied entirely on love and rejected all use of force, and if it had asserted its right and duty to secure a fair field for this religion as for all other religions which were consistent with law, order, and the rights of all its subjects, India would have accepted the announcement with confidence and respect. Such a declaration would probably not have raised substantially the ideals or social standards of India. But it would have removed uneasiness and inspired the reverence always accorded by the East to strength, lofty ideals, and sincerity. India has never persecuted her prophets though she has seldom followed them for long. Gautama, Asoka, Akbar, and Gandhi may have failed to perpetuate their influence on the succeeding generations. But they never aroused violent opposition or suspicious hatred. This was reserved for Aurungzeb who tried to destroy by force a religion for which he provided no convincing spiritual equivalent, and for the British Government which by its nervous vacillation had created a feeling of insecurity.

When Asoka enforced his edicts, which are recorded on the pillars that consecrate his memory, he roused no feeling of revolt, because they were recognised as the expression of Buddha's ideals and the inevitable results of his attitude towards life. Similarly the suppression of infanticide and suttee was accepted as a recognition of the equal value of every living soul in the eyes of God, a truth that is specially emphasised by Christ, but was not hidden from the many saints and reformers of India. And the rise of Indian Christian communities, from which the possibility of caste or idolatry has been excluded by the spirit which inspires them, has never shocked or alarmed India. But it was hard to understand or trust a Government which emphasised its aloofness from all religion, which sometimes went out of its way to pamper religious prejudice and intolerance, and which was apparently seeking by its schools and institutions to undermine all usages that hindered its material advancement.

The Queen's proclamation of 1858 which brought this unhappy business to an end was in the tradition and manner of Asoka and Constantine. It recognised the conclusions and met the difficulties that the preceding paragraphs have tried to formulate. There was nothing in it which had not at various times and in fragmentary utterances been enunciated by the British Parliament, the Directors and their agents in India. But it reaffirmed and summarised them in a convincing and stately manner, providing an appropriate shrine for the charter whereby alone we can hope to retain our connection with India. That it had personally been approved by the great Queen and substantially amended by her own hand inspired India with a confidence which no Directors' despatch, nor even an Act of Parliament, could have produced. And the Queen's servants in India, as they had now become, found clearly enunciated at last the principles for which, as servants of the Company, they had so long been groping.

In the face of all India, as Lawrence and Edwardes had urged, the Queen declared herself the head of a Christian nation. 'Firmly relying on the truth of Christianity and acknowledging with gratitude the solace of religion', this nation once again and finally disclaimed through its Queen, 'the right and desire to impose our convictions on any of our subjects'. The ambiguous and degrading term 'Neutrality', was by the Queen's hand erased from the draft. How can a Government which adheres to one religion alone be 'neutral'? Tolerant it can and will be. And 'toleration' became henceforth 'the badge of all our tribe in India'. None was to be favoured, molested, or disquieted by reason of his religion. Equal and impartial protection under the law was assured to all. Those in authority were precluded from interference with any religious belief or worship. That God, the Father of all, would help England to observe and India to profit by these principles was the sincere conviction of the ruler who closed this Christian-hearted proclamation by a reference to His power and inspiration. It was not surprising that Christian missions joined with leaders of Hindu and Mohammedan thought in cordial expression of gratitude.

The response generally of the official world in India was appropriate. In the days of the Mutiny there had been hours when even Christian-spirited men showed signs of faltering. Canning, sorely tried and attacked on all sides, showed his sensitiveness to Ellenborough's criticism by stopping for the time his subscriptions to mission work. He rejected an offer of organised help from the Indian Christian community and postponed for some time the day of humiliation and intercession proposed by the Christian churches. But meanwhile Pfander was not only allowed but urged by Punjab officials to continue his street preaching in Peshawar. And before the final restoration of peace officials in all parts of India were beginning to employ and attract to government service the Indian Christians who had stood so well the hour of trial. Gone for ever were the days when such candidates were eyed with disfavour or expressly excluded. Elphinstone throughout the period in Bombay had been in close touch and frequent consultation with missionary Wilson. Without anxiety he despatched all his troops to the troubled areas and his usual subscriptions to the missions societies. It was left for Lawrence, who continued for a time to serve the Province he had kept so loyal, to be the first official of standing to begin an official ceremony with a Christian prayer.

That toleration was not only compatible with religious devotion but a necessary feature of Christianity was shown by Lawrence's refusal to destroy the Pearl Mosque at Agra, as was suggested by advocates of stern reprisal methods, or to hand over the mosques at Delhi and Lahore to Christian communities. Reprisals elsewhere were often savage and calculated to rouse in India a feeling that is not even now quite dead. It is not for us who were spared the sights and tales that evoked such punishment to cast a stone. We can at least with pride remember that it was the spirit of Lawrence rather than of Hodson[1] that survived the first storm of angry passion. There was more general tolerance of Indian modes of life and worship, though less submission to what was morally harmful in them, among Europeans, ecclesiastical as well as lay, in India after the Mutiny than there was before.

In England the Mutiny created a feeling of humiliation and failure which found expression in a vigorous determination to advance more effective measures for India's enlightenment. There was no talk of suppression of such activities as might increase the power and energy of our Indian subjects. Their rulers were urged to expedite all arrangements for the universities which had already been sanctioned. The Christian Literature Society owes its origin to a widespread desire, evoked by the Mutiny, to bring more light and understanding to India. 'Consecrated cobblers' and 'Psalm-singing generals' came at last to their own and their share in seeking to avert and helping to alleviate the disaster was recognised by a generation that had been taught by Dickens and Thackeray to regard them with amused surprise.

It was Edmund Burke who first aroused the conscience of England in Indian affairs. Our period ends in a clearer recognition of his maxim. 'Magnanimity in politics[2] is not seldom the truest wisdom, and a great

[1] Indian cavalry leader and subordinate of John Lawrence. On his shooting of the Mogul princes near Delhi see histories of Indian Mutiny.

[2] From Burke's speech for conciliation with the colonies, 1775.

empire and little minds go ill together. We ought to elevate our minds to the greatness of that trust to which the order of Providence has called us.' The same note was sounded by the greatest Indian ruler of pre-Mutiny days. 'To fear God and to have no other fear'[1] is a maxim of which the truth and wisdom are proved day by day in politics.

[1] From a minute of Lord Dalhousie on the provision of suitable instruction for Christian sepoys. Quoted in Lee Warner's *Life of the Marquis of Dalhousie*.

PART FOUR

1857–1920

PART IV—1858–1920

CHAPTER XV

HARMONIOUS CO-OPERATION

Proclamation of 1858—compared with Edict of Milan—toleration and open profession of faith—official testimony to missions—smouldering controversy—support of missions by officers and civil servants—a satisfactory settlement—missions in Indian states—legal status of Indian Christians—recognition of Sunday—mission approval of Government attitude—their identification with Government—and with western civilisation—its origin and dangers—possible loss of spiritual power—merging of mission schools in Government system—administrative work of missions—their political attitude—merchants and missions—the Long case—attacks on missions—growth of mutual goodwill.

THE Queen's Proclamation of 1858 introduces a period in which Christianity in India occupied a position similar in many respects to that assigned to the Church by Constantine's Edict of Milan.[1] Christianity remained firmly established, as it was from the Edict of Milan up to the time of Theodosius, as one among many religions recognised and protected by the State; *de facto* if not *de jure* it became the most favoured religion in so far as it was the professed religion of the supreme authority, identified in the public mind with many of the functions of government and freely applied by the Government, whose conscience unofficially was in its charge, in philanthropic schemes and measures for the moral and material welfare of India. It is creditable to

[1] 'Let those in error equally enjoy peace and rest with the faithful. Let none molest his neighbour. We have the glorious abode of truth. We wish for others, that in community of mind with us they may share in our joys.'

(*Translation of part of Edict of Milan*)

the head and heart of its leaders that it made no attempt during the period to secure for itself the monopoly that Theodosius bestowed in the Catholic Church. Its general attitude was such as to arouse no resentment in the more enlightened circles of other communities and to stimulate what deserved to survive in their cults rather than to extinguish them.

Times were indeed changed when a Prime Minister[1] not noted for ecclesiastical zeal, two years after the Mutiny, could say in public, 'It is not only our duty, but in our own interests, to promote the diffusion of Christianity as far as possible throughout the length and breadth of India'. To which the Secretary of State for India appended the statement that 'every additional[2] Christian is an additional bond of union with this country and an additional source of strength to the Empire'.

Throughout the period the chorus of official praise and benediction swelled in volume and intensity. John Lawrence's tribute of praise at the close of his Indian career was of course to be expected. For India's welfare 'the missions have done more than all other agencies combined'. Lord Reay,[3] introducing to the Prince of Wales in 1876 a deputation of Indian Christians, who in other stages of the royal tour had been by official oversight ignored, said that 'they were doing for India more than all those civilians, soldiers, judges and governors whom Your Highness has met'. Sir Charles Elliott[4] in 1891 happily described their work as 'an unrecognised and unofficial branch of the great movement that alone justifies British rule in Asia'. Sir Mackworth Young[5] a few years later called them the

[1] Lord Palmerston.
[2] Charles Wood.
[3] Governor of Bombay, 1873.
[4] Lieut.-Governor of Bengal.
[5] Lieut.-Governor of the Punjab.

most potent force in India. Lord Curzon devoted some of his most effective phrases to the missionaries who had stood for months 'between the dead and the living' during the great famine of his viceroyalty. The tale of tribute could be indefinitely prolonged. There were few men in authority indeed during the period who did not testify in public to India's need of Christ's spirit and Christ's disciples.

It was too much of course to expect that all signs of nervous apprehension would disappear at once from an official world responsible for law and order in a country renowned for explosive fanaticism. For some years the old and troublesome question of proselytism by officials acting in their private capacity continued to vex the council table. Lord Stanley[1] in the House of Commons declared that it was perilous for men in authority to do as individuals that which they officially disclaim. But simultaneously Charles Trevelyan in Madras was assuring his subordinates that they had this private right to recommend by all proper means their respective religions. The Government of India in a comprehensive resolution censured a Commissioner, Deputy-Commissioner and Colonel for attending the baptism of six C.M.S. converts, and remonstrated with officers of the 24th Punjabi Regiment who referred 'enquiries' in their company to the local mission and continued their instructions when the regiment moved to a station where professional instruction could not be found. But Montgomery, ruler of the province, supported the Bishop of Calcutta[2] in his protest, and Charles Wood, who by this time had succeeded doubting Stanley, once again emphasised the private rights of all officers, civil or military, and gave to missionaries the right of access to Christian sepoys in their lines, as well as to non-Christian sepoys the right

[1] Later 15th Earl of Derby; Secretary of State for India.

[2] Bishop Cotton.

of receiving instruction outside their lines. These orders have never since been questioned. And it would be ungracious and misleading to dwell on other instances of official fussiness arising out of excessive regard for non-Christian feeling. As time went on they became steadily fewer in number, and because of their isolation perhaps more conspicuous.

The position of Christian missions in the protected Indian States naturally presented delicate questions that required on both sides the tactful handling that as a rule it received. The publication of any general ruling on the subject was characteristically avoided. But it would be true to say generally that, while the Indian rulers have been ready to accord to Christian missionaries the same rights that all subjects of their state enjoy under conditions guaranteed by the supreme government, missionaries on their side have been careful to remember that they are propagating a faith which is not that of the ruler of the land, and have been tactful and chary in their references to the supreme government. The relations that existed between Schwartz and the Raja of Tanjore have been emulated in many instances, and rulers with the prestige of Holkar of Indore have not hesitated to attend public disputations between missionaries and pundits. The advice given by the Lieutenant-General of the N.W. Provinces, when the Rajputana missions were formed, has received wide acceptance. 'These gentlemen cannot be interfered with. All that can be done is to beg them to be undemonstrative in their operations, and to exercise their functions unobtrusively and with discretion.'

In safeguarding the legal rights and status of Indian Christians the principles outlined and partially translated into action by Bentinck and Dalhousie in the preceding period were carried to their logical conclusions. Sir Henry Maine said, on introducing the Bill regulating the re-marriage of native converts, 'We will not force any man to be a Christian ; we will not even tempt him to become one. But if he chooses to be a Christian we will protect him in those rights of conscience which we have been the first to introduce into this country and will apply to him those principles of equal dealing between man and man of which we are in India the sole depositories '. By 1866 all attempts to tie converts to Hindu wives who deserted them had been defeated by a measure which satisfied the claims of justice and the teaching of St. Paul, episcopally interpreted. Attacks on the previously established right of converts to their property and inheritance had been resisted and the same right had been maintained in Indian states.

Gone for ever were the days when governors incurred the Directors' censure for drinking parties during divine service, or when Chaplain Brown recalled to the table a Governor-General who had forgotten grace. What Wellesley had partially succeeded in enforcing, and even Teignmouth, despite his memories of Clapham, had been too weary to fight for, was now accomplished. The highest in the land drove in official state to church, while sabbatical peace prevailed in their cutcherries. It was John Lawrence, as Chief Commissioner in the Punjab, and then as Viceroy over all India, who insisted on this reminder that he represented a Christian Queen. Nor did the Prince of Wales forget the fact during his Indian tour of 1875–6. The official world accepted gleefully the larger measure of repose gained by the Christian observance of Sunday and the tolerant retention of Hindu and Islamic holy days.

What has been recorded above suggests that the British Government during the period under review, freed from nervous scruples about its association with the Christian faith, offered a fair field and all necessary protection and opportunities for mission work. This was the general conclusion reached in the report of the

International Conference of missions which examined carefully at Edinburgh in 1910 the attitude of Government missions in all parts of the world. It was cordially endorsed by all representatives of American missions in India. Missions are no freer than other communities from the desire to criticise. The authorities do not escape occasional censure in their report. But their impartial administration of the law, their obvious desire that the Indian convert should have fair play, the freedom allowed in all branches of their work and the encouragement and financial support bestowed on much of it were gratefully acknowledged and contrasted with the treatment at that time accorded in a few other parts of the British empire and in several of the French colonies. The Government's refusal officially to support propaganda work was recognised as inevitable, and was wisely welcomed by most of the witnesses and speakers as ultimately conducive to the welfare of genuine Christianity. There was no explicit desire for relations such as were reported from the Dutch East Indies, where the Dutch precedent in Ceylon was followed, to the extent at least that religious work was openly recognised and supported, and even to some extent organised, by the Government who maintained a special officer to keep them in touch with mission work. Whatever may be the advantages of such relations, they prevent that disentanglement of evangelical work from politics and racial questions which is rightly valued in India and is attributed partly to the aloofness of the official world. There was in fact a tendency at the Edinburgh Conference, which was intensified at the Jerusalem Conference of 1928, to deprecate any kind of identification of mission work with the official administration of a country. To what extent such identification has come into being and is to be regretted in India is a question that calls for discussion at this point.

HARMONIOUS CO-OPERATION

During a school inspection in India the present writer was surprised to hear what he understood to be the word 'missions' included in a list of exports from England to India that formed part of a geography lesson. Subsequent enquiry revealed that the word in the pupil's mind, but mispronounced, was 'machines'. 'The difference is slight', said the teacher with oriental tact. For missionaries like machinery are instruments of western civilisation which has made India what it is.' What these civilising forces had made of India he did not proceed to specify. But the incident started a train of thought which has persisted ever since in the writer's mind.

'If any army', said Keshab Chandar Sen,[1] 'holds India for England, it is the army of Christian missionaries'. Bishop Cotton on his arrival in India was 'agreeably surprised' by the place occupied in the official world by missionaries. Though it was true that 'some of them studied the book of Revelation more than the Koran and Shastras', they were 'sensible and practical in their work to a degree that I had not expected'. Following in fact the example set by Schwartz and Carey, Duff and Wilson, and these men had Pauline authority for their policy, Christian missionaries by the close of our period had proved their usefulness to Government in many spheres of administration. As pioneers in science and exploration, as experts in sociology and languages, as managers of schools and colleges and leaders in the academic world, as superintendents of hospitals and far-famed surgeons, as chairmen of municipal councils and presidents of district boards, as mediators between Government and the people, as information bureaux on local culture and traditions, and as moulders of public opinion, they had come to be regarded almost as philan-

[1] Hindu reformer; at one time a leader in Brahmo Samaj; broke away to found a separate sect. The reference is to a lecture in 1866.

thropic and expert agents of Government in the work of civilisation. In some parts philanthropic schemes such as the maintenance of leper asylums and reclamation of criminal tribes had definitely been assigned by Government to missions. In most parts the task of educating the depressed classes fell mainly to the same agencies. In all parts the withdrawal, towards the end of the period, of mission schools and colleges from the educational system, would have disorganised the whole system, imposed an intolerable burden on the provincial exchequer, and excited widespread discontent. Proposals on financial or other grounds to close mission high schools or colleges invariably produced petitions and memorials from communities and individuals that had no ostensible claim on the institutions except residence among those who had come to regard it as an established amenity.

There has always been a popular tendency in India to associate every important event and movement, whether good or evil, with the British Government. During the period under review its operations were in fact so impressive and far-reaching that they seemed to absorb a great deal that in the more complex and elaborate western states is sharply differentiated. The process of absorption was often unconscious and sometimes in opposition to the express policy of Government. Public opinion anyhow attributed to the official world a comprehensive and digestive capacity resembling that of the whale in mythology. What is good for the whale may be dangerous for Jonah. And there are some who suspect that Christian missions may have lost some force from a process to which the Government and its subjects have certainly owed very much. It is possible that emphatic co-operation with a Government that represented western civilisation invested missions in the eyes of the people with the functions of a western and cultural agency rather than with those of a spiritual power that recognises no geographical or cultural distinctions.

It is true that Schwartz, Carey, and Duff never hesitated to devote their time and energy to the assistance of Government in any work of charity or enlightenment. But this was in days when the line of cleavage between missionary and official was always discernible and sometimes emphatic. A man like Carey, who had defied the authorities and preached without license in the bazaar at the risk of his life, stood out as an evangelist even when he had become a professor in Fort William College. Moreover the sphere of official action was not nearly so comprehensive in the first half of the nineteenth century as it became in post-Mutiny days.

Nor do we forget that Christ's life was no less important than His teaching and that this life was lived in the world and devoted in generous measure to the material needs of others. But this ministry was the inevitable result of a nature wholly inspired by divine love. Far from suggesting to onlookers the importance of the material world it attracted attention to its own spiritual origin. Those who watched the Healer at work had no doubt at all that He possessed also the unique gift of forgiveness of sins and bestowal of spiritual power, or that He attached far more importance to this direct sign of His Father's grace than to the material benefits that were, if not merely a by-product, a comparatively insignificant corollary.

In suggesting that this was not the impression produced in India by mission work of the second half of the nineteenth century we do not mean to imply that the missionaries individually ever forgot the essentially spiritual nature of their work. But it is hard to believe that the majority of them, immersed, so far as the outside world could judge, in activities resembling greatly those of the local self-government, medical, and educational officers of the district, created in any but those who came into close and daily contact with them a sense of concentrated spiritual power. It would be harder still to cite the name of any missionary who meant spiritually to the Indian world at large all that is implied in the memory of Tukaram[1] or Kabir[2] or Gandhi, as he was before his fatal entanglement in the network of political compromise and economic speculation. India is always looking for a prophet. It is to spiritual forces alone that all that is bad in caste and the social life of India will eventually yield. Christianity regarded merely as a feature of western civilisation may disintegrate, but it will never edify, society. Standing out as the dominant motive force in every type of progressive civilisation, it will bring freedom, not from the social obligations of caste, which is what western civilisation means to most, but from its antisocial and reactionary tendencies.

Nowhere has the loss of distinctively spiritual characteristics, in the eyes of the outside world, been more marked than in the higher educational activities of Christian missions. The present writer has had special and frequent opportunities of observing the spiritual effect of their schools and colleges on Christian pupils who have enjoyed all the privileges of their hostel and community life, and on Hindus and Mohammedans who have been lucky enough to come into personal daily contact with the Christian elements in their staff. But it is certain that to many of their pupils and pupils' parents, and to almost all external observers, these institutions have presented themselves as offering the same attractions and following the same aims as Government schools and colleges. The latter owe their title

[1] Popular and religious Marathi poet of 17th century.
[2] The mystic weaver poet of north India; 15th century.

of 'model' institutions to the financial resources at their disposal. Mission institutions, on the other hand, charge lower fees and often have more European instructors on the staff. Bible instruction though usually compulsory is tactfully inserted. That it is a by-product rather than an integral part of the curriculum is suggested by its total exclusion from the courses presented at the government or university inspection and the corresponding certificate or degree examinations. During the latter part of the nineteenth century at all events it would have been possible for a student of such an institution to secure the highest degree in English literature or European history without any conception of the fundamentally Christian basis of these subjects.

Nothing was explicitly surrendered by missions when they accepted their incorporation in the system formulated by the 1854 despatch. Undoubtedly Duff and Wilson thought that such an incorporation saved the system as a whole from the reproach of 'godlessness' implied otherwise by the exclusion of the Bible from Government institutions. Freedom from religious restrictions of every kind was expressly secured ; not until the end of the period, and then only in a hesitating way, was the right of enforcing religious instruction ever questioned. The questions when they did come were inspired by abstract theory and a desire to imitate the West rather than by any antagonism to Christianity. But the reluctance of Government to withdraw educationally in favour of missions was not foreseen. Nor was it possible to forecast the rapid development of social self-government with its inevitable accompaniment of secular education. The Hunter Education Commission appointed by Lord Ripon in 1882 reaffirmed effectively the claims of aided as against government institutions. But it is doubtful whether the three mission representatives foresaw clearly the rapid growth of a type of aided school that was no less secular, and far more indifferent to character building, than the Government school. Between these two types of institutions the essentially spiritual aims of the third type ceased to arouse popular imagination.

As a result India to-day has a Hindu and a Mohammedan university;[1] it has no Christian university nor system of Christian schools and colleges. That such a university would have aroused official or religious opposition, or that the Government would necessarily refuse recognition or aid to a system independent of its own system, but morally and socially quite as acceptable, is a proposition that few would maintain. No such proposal emerged during the period under review because of the prominence assigned to the task of 'leavening the lump'. It is always dangerous to let a single parable dictate a policy. Mixture of metaphors is sometimes a safeguard. Mission leaders in India have not always remembered that they are 'the salt of the earth' and as such subject to peculiar dangers.

In the difficult and occasionally ambiguous position attained through their wholehearted co-operation in some spheres of official work the missions deserve throughout the period great credit for their general determination to hold aloof from political and racial controversy. For two reasons this was difficult and at times distasteful. To refuse official nominations to legislative councils and local government bodies would have deprived them of opportunities of supporting measures of social and moral importance, and the Government of their expert advice. As official nominees of these bodies it was ungracious, if not always impossible, to refuse support to the Government even on controversial matters where no definitely Christian principle was involved. The inevitable result has been an impres-

[1] At Benares and Aligarh. Charters given within the last twenty years.

sion, confined it must be added to those not personally acquainted with missionaries, that the Christian standpoint is essentially European and official.

On the other hand chivalry and Christianity grow up side by side. Sympathy with the weaker side and a desire to help the 'under dog' have always been associated with the Anglo-Saxon Christian, with results at times more creditable to heart than head. 'Imperialism' is a term unfashionable in Christian circles to-day. A man who is subject to strong religious emotion finds it easier to see the point of view of the races not yet entrusted with power than to sympathise with those who find themselves unable to surrender that power to others.

There must have been many missionaries during the troubled years that close our period who felt a strong desire to take their stand with Mr. Gandhi. He had undoubtedly inspired India and individual Indians with a sense of national dignity and personal responsibility. Such a fact was in itself Christian. More than this, 'he turned the eyes of India to the Cross', he quickened interest in the personality of Christ; 'for the first time in Indian history a nation for the attainment of its ends substituted suffering for force'. Such words are a generous but just appreciation of the Mahatma and his followers during an all too short but glorious stage in his career. In 1921 'no man in India had so many followers'. No man perhaps had ever had so many followers simultaneously, and like their master, in jail. At one time it seemed possible that complete abstention from alcohol and a breaking of the tyranny of caste, rather than violence, and confusion of thought and action, would issue from his spiritual rule.

An instinctive desire for communion with such a man was enhanced by the appeal indirectly conveyed to missionaries through criticism of their work and attitude. While ready to admit that they had wished the good of

India, that they had tried to act justly and had generally succeeded, Mr. Gandhi accused them of not 'trying sufficiently to enter into the Indian mind'. The organ of the Servants of India Society,[1] a body entitled to a respectful hearing, noted that 'while it is natural to expect missionaries to be the intermediaries between the custodians of privilege and the exponents of reform, actually most of them are lukewarm or hostile to us'. There was a widespread feeling that they lacked 'racial humility' and that their 'impartiality' meant identification with the privileged party. There were missionaries who attributed a contemporary falling off in the number of high caste converts and in the sale of Bibles to criticism such as this. Undoubtedly the attitude of educated India towards missions has become more critical, and perhaps in the end more helpful, since the beginning of the Swaraj movement. But the criticism has had no connection with Hindu or Islamic orthodoxy and can be met, to some extent has been met, without any surrender of genuinely Christian principles.

The mission world in general was strong and wise enough to resist these appeals to feeling and interests. One of its most attractive and inspiring representatives had dissociated himself from mission work, though in no sense from the principles which in his opinion ought to direct it, before assuming an active part in political controversy. Missionaries as a body abstained from any action of a spectacular or emotional nature, and in so doing gained on a long view what they may have lost for the time in prestige and popularity.

It was not only that the most clear-sighted among them mistrusted Mr. Gandhi's head as fully as they admired his heart. They realised of course his inability

[1] Founded by Ghokhale for the social and economic amelioration of India. Its members are pledged to poverty and whole-time service of India.

to appreciate and interpret facts and anticipated the conclusion, to which he himself was driven later, that he was 'incapable of controlling and disciplining the spirit that he had roused'. And most of them had been taught by history and experience that in all political and racial questions there is truth and justice on both sides. It is the statesman's task to choose between them and the historian's to weigh them in the balance. But he whose essential task it is to feed and stimulate the spiritual life will maintain a post from which he can assist both sides to concentrate attention on what is spiritually sound and defensible in their positions. That such assistance was given to both sides during the critical years that close our period is certain ; there are some who regret that it was not rendered in a more public and authoritative manner.

But there was something else, far more vital and fundamental than all these considerations, that encouraged the missions in their quietest attitude and was responsible for the general approval of such an attitude by the Edinburgh conference of missions in its 1910 study of the whole subject. There was a genuine conviction that not only the association of the Christian churches with political parties, but also their preoccupation with political questions, is not in accord with the mind and spirit of Christ revealed in the Gospels. St. Paul's manifest respect for the Roman empire and interest in its organisation undoubtedly influenced the early development of Christianity and may have facilitated its close alliance with the State from the fourth century onwards. When Church and State again became distinguishable there was for some time a tendency on the Church's part to ally itself with a particular party of the State. After the Church in England had withdrawn from its association with the Tories there were signs throughout the nineteenth century of political preoccupation among many of the Christian bodies in the land. Against all this there was a reaction which was felt during the first quarter of the present century in India. Attempts to justify political economic theories by Bible quotations were given up by men who found in Christ a spiritual leader completely unmoved by the burning political questions of his day. 'To Caesar the things that are Caesar's' came to be interpreted as implying a dismissal from the mind of all that has no place in a scheme of real values. Christ's kingdom was not of this (material) world, and though his disciples were to live in it they were to concentrate their efforts exclusively on making it more conscious of the real or spiritual world. Whether consciousness of that world would affect the course of the other was not answered by Christ. It is arguable that the question would not have interested him. Such anyhow was the feeling that helped many missionaries to hold their hands when political and racial passion was aflame in India. Their aloofness was assisted by the fact that no schemes for the social or moral improvement of India were the monopoly of either side in the contest. Of Mr. Gandhi it could be said that he was advocating with all his heart social measures that the Government had long before him adopted and, with mission help, attempted to carry out.

Passing from the political and racial sphere to that of economics we enter on a field where it was perhaps more difficult and more dangerous for Christian bodies to remain silent. With the development of industry and commerce, and the rapid growth of an unofficial mercantile and industrial European community in India, economic questions became urgent and the possibility of strife more urgent. With Indian labour almost illiterate and inarticulate and wholly unorganised there seemed to be a clear call for unofficial bodies, without selfish interests and animated by Christian charity, to mediate between such workers and employers who were often pathetically ignorant of the life and traditions of those on whom their wealth depended. If missions did not undertake such work there was, towards the end of our period, a real danger that the workers' cause would be taken up by agencies that saw in such agitation an opportunity of advancing political or racial interests.

The situation was complicated by the changes that were transforming Anglo-Indian society. The removal of all restrictions on immigration in the preceding period and the opportunities for commercial and industrial development had brought to India a large number of Europeans of all grades. English society was no longer a united homogeneous body. It was large enough to split up into official and non-official groups. The growing frequency of visits home also discouraged solidarity of feeling. A situation was reached not unlike that which disturbed the last years of the Roman Republic, when the wealth was in the hands of the mercantile community, and prestige and political power lay with a handful of officials.

The situation was eased when the growth of legislative councils and local self-government gave openings to the merchants for administrative and legislative responsibility and opportunities for friendly co-operation with officials and missionaries.

Prior to this there had undoubtedly been times when they tended to eye the other two classes suspiciously as leagued against them. More particularly they feared, as employers of labour in the early stages of industrial development are prone to do, the effect of education, such as official and mission agencies were combining to provide, on their supply of labour and its quality. Bitterness increased in periods like that of 1865–1870, when a boom in cotton produced feverish speculation and subsequent financial disaster.

In these circumstances it behoved missions to walk warily. For the most part they seem to have done so. There was indeed in the early part of the period a *cause célèbre* when a missionary, John Long, was fined and imprisoned for inflaming racial feeling in connection with labour unrest on some indigo plantations in Bengal. The facts of the case are difficult to ascertain. The substance of the offence seems to have been the translation into English and publication of a Bengali play which depicted vividly the woes of the coolies and the conditions of indigo labour. There seems some reason to suppose that the offending missionary thought that he was acting in accordance with the wishes of Government. The case anyhow is sufficiently isolated to suggest that opportunities for mercantile reprisals were rare. That feeling existed is shown by attacks that were made generally on mission work in some European circles during part of the period. In 1887 a determined assault was delivered by no less a person than an Anglican Canon in the Church Congress and *Fortnightly Review*.[1] Missionaries were condemned as persons of inferior qualifications, living in comfortable and expensive bungalows, attending to everything except their proper work and producing in return for a large outlay a small handful of unsatisfactory converts. In 1872 Archbishop Tait's request for a general day of intercession for missions met with a distinctly cold press. A leading article in *The Times*, referring to this 'fatuous and useless observance', asked for a public exhibition of missionaries and converts. 'An ordinary Englishman has seen almost every human or brute native of foreign climes. But few can say they have seen a missionary or Christian convert. . . .' The Archbishop's rebuke in a private letter to Delane was all that the situation required. 'My fear for the world is that through the vast influence

[1] Canon Isaac Taylor.

of the press we may be governed by boys and those not wise ones!'

Attacks such as these were not characteristic of English opinion which became steadily more favourable to missions during the period. They were clearly inspired by interested persons outside England with a superficial knowledge of mission activities and interests to which they thought them opposed. In India anyhow the official world was not responsible. They reflected probably a feeling in unofficial and particularly industrial circles which has steadily been improved by the tact and caution of missions and the increasing knowledge of their work and aims gained from association with them on government committees and in philanthropic work. It is improbable that planter and missionary will ever regard education from the same standpoint. The stories that they tell against one another will continue for long to enliven India. But on the whole the policy suggested at the Edinburgh conference has prevailed to the good of all parties. Economic like political questions usually have two sides. It is the business of missionaries to interest each side in the other side's point of view. Not dissuading their converts from asserting their legal rights, and not necessarily abstaining from appeals to Government in support of such rights, they have most carefully to resist the suggestion that Christians as such have any peculiar rights and to encourage the idea that their religion helps and requires them to respect the rights of others. In accordance with this policy missions were at no time during the period conspicuous for industrial intervention. On several occasions and notably during the Champaran[1] agrarian disputes Mr. Gandhi, without suspicion of self-interest, took on himself work and anxiety that some critics thought would have been

[1] An area in Bihar. The dispute between European planters and local labour was ultimately investigated and settled by the Government.

appropriate to a Christian community. The mission reply would probably be that in such matters Government has not shown itself averse from Christian influence and that its intervention has usually been timely and effective.

CHAPTER XVI

THE FRUITS OF CO-OPERATION

Christianity concerned with character, not codes—influence on admini stration steady, not spectacular—pace regulated by growth of publi opinion and education—survival of religious fanaticism—absence o active opposition to missions—discreet attitude of missions to India religions—no wish to denationalize—growing acceptance of Christia principles by non-Christians—the Bombay Vaishnavite case—mission aries no longer in foreground—tactful co-operation in social reform— marriage laws and customs—orthodox position and its evil results— ameliorative legislation—supported by enlightened Hindus—reactionar arguments—Hindu modes of thought—civil marriage—efforts for th depressed classes—public opinion too strong for regulations—campaig against obscenity—temple prostitution—cruelty to animals—penal cod and prisons—treatment of lepers.

FROM the effect on mission work of its contact wit the official world we turn to signs of the influenc exerted on the Government by the spiritual forces whic the Christian agencies in India represented.

Christianity had produced in the western world n so much a new code of morals as a type of charact endowed with sufficient driving power to translate in legislative and administrative action principles that ha already commended themselves in theory to the noble representatives of other philosophies and religion Even those who find nothing uniquely distinctive in th Christian code of ethics admit that the Christian fait pre-eminently inspires an attempt to regulate the rela tions of men to men by this standard. Unlike mos other religions, and in special contrast with Hinduism it affords no sanction for conduct that falls far short o the highest ideals of the age. It cannot like Hinduism be adapted to the demands of selfishness or lust.

This type of character in the western world slowly but urely humanised social institutions and economic relaions ; with special emphasis on the rights and value of ach individual soul, it abolished slavery and secured or women fair and honourable treatment. We have lready seen it at work in India from 1813 to 1857. What results can it show in our present period to be compared with the abolition of suttee and measures gainst infanticide ?

We must expect results less spectacular and striking han those of the preceding period. It is always the first stages in the moral and social uplifting of a nation hat are most dramatic. Much remained still to be done n 1857. And of this very much is even yet undone, even unattempted. But the evils that remained were not such as impressed themselves forcibly on the Christian mind, like suttee or infanticide or sacrificial murder. Many of them were hidden from all but the expert and vigilant western observer, being bound up with that side of domestic and social life which reveals itself only to hose outsiders who insist on penetrating below the surface.

Moreover the growing tendency of the period was to associate Indians more and more with the work of Government. Reform was often postponed, not from fear of orthodox discontent or fanatical uprising, but from a desire to make Indian thought and feeling a partner in the great enterprise. The standpoint of John Lawrence was inevitably left behind. No longer could the British Government overrule all objections by a proclamation such as his when the question of Bible teaching in schools was under discussion. 'We have not been elected by the people, but we are here through our moral superiority, by the force of circumstances, and the will of Providence. This alone constitutes our charter to govern India. In doing the best we can for the people we are bound by our conscience and not by theirs.'[1] Such worc were more appropriate to the times of Wellesley an Bentinck, when India had not yet awoken from he moral and intellectual sleep, than to those of Dalhousi Ripon, and Curzon, when education had aroused wi and conscience, and political concessions had stimulate some feeling at least of responsibility and power. Ther was more recognition too in the seats of the mighty c the brighter and more elevating side of Indian religio than there was in Lawrence's time. Officials had com to realise that a country and a religion which had throw up periodically such saints and reformers as the Buddh and Ramanuja Chariar might in the future co-operat to secure by consent what force could only ineffectuall attempt. It was worth while to wait. And often i fact we did wait. The courage and resolution of Bentinck or Dalhousie were not found wanting when th evil was so urgent and the remedy so clear that postpone ment would have been a crime. But these occasion necessarily became fewer as the years passed by.

There were constant reminders that religious fanaticisn was still a force to be reckoned with by all reformers 'Religion in danger' was a cry with which unscrupulou opponents of the Government could always creat embarrassment or delay consideration of reforms affectin vested interests. The murder of Lord Mayo[2] by fanatical Afghan convict, the riots in connection with th Benares waterworks and the Bombay anti-plague regula tions of 1898, and the Khilafat agitation of 1921 showe how religious passion can be aroused in an illiterat population by those who desire unrest. The communa animosity between Hindu and Mohammedan, far fron

[1] From a minute of John Lawrence on the question of religious in struction in schools of the Punjab.

[2] Viceroy, 1869–1872. Murdered on his visit to the Andaman Island by a fanatical Afghan convict.

equiring any outside stimulus to keep it alive, was onstantly manifesting its existence by riots that leaders of the communities found themselves powerless to vert.

But this fanaticism was seldom directed against pecifically Christian teaching or against legislative or xecutive acts obviously inspired by Christian principles. The absence of any widespread or intense feeling against Christianity as such is difficult to explain, when one onsiders its growth since 1857. It is true that the last ensus of 1921 showed only 1½ per cent of the whole population as Christian. Though they number in all more than four and a half millions there is only one Christian to twenty-two Mohammedans and sixty-eight Hindus. But there has been a steady increase in the ate of progress. During the last recorded decade the ncrease has exceeded 100,000 a year. In south India nd parts of Bombay the Indian Christian community is numerically important and in all lines of life conspicuous. In every part of India leaders of the community are occupying positions of trust and importance. The change effected by Christianity in the lives and status of he depressed classes has excited general comment.

The opposition excited by this success during the atter part of our period usually took the salutary form of an attempt to imitate the activities of Christian bodies, nd thereby to make them less indispensable to the uplifting of India and the depressed classes in particular. The Arya Samaj,[1] which took the lead in the reformation of Hinduism on orthodox lines, and occasionally in the prosecution of Christian-spirited enterprise, undoubtedly went further at times and showed in speech and action hostility to Christians as represented by the West. A Census superintendent suggests that an attempt was

[1] Founded in 1874 for the reform of Hinduism on Vedic principles; 468,000 adherents, mainly in north India, in 1921.

made in places by its agents to induce Indian Christians to describe themselves as Hindu in the census returns. But even here the bitterness was probably in origin and essence racial rather than religious.

For the absence of religious opposition a reason may perhaps be found in the growing knowledge of the personality of Christ and reverence for his characteristics. This knowledge, often inadequate and rarely supported by any historical feeling, but none the less emotionally real, has been promulgated by many non-Christian leaders of thought and sentiment in India as well as by mission schools and colleges. Another reason is undoubtedly the general tendency of missions to abandon the vigorous iconoclasm of Duff and many of the earliest missionaries. There is noticeable in their literature and preaching a growing humility, a readiness to recognise what is spiritually great in Hinduism and Islam and to build on it, a desire to co-operate with the pure in heart of all religions in the great warfare against materialism. And above all they are beginning to convince India that Christianity is not a western import, but something that grows naturally in any soil and in a form appropriate to that soil. That a follower of Christ is thereby denationalised is no longer seriously believed by thoughtful Indians.

These tendencies, which were gradually being developed during our period, strengthened the hand of Government in its social and moral work. It was often found necessary to postpone legislation on the grounds that it was in advance of the times and liable to be misunderstood or misinterpreted by the ignorant or malicious. But it became possible for the Government without fear of criticism or resentment to take its stand on admittedly Christian principles, with the conviction openly expressed that these principles were universally recognised by educated men and accepted by men of good will irrespective of race or religion.

As early as 1862 the community of feeling between non-Christian reformers and a Christian Government found striking expression in a judgment of the High Court of Bombay. A fierce attack in an organ of the social reform movement on the 'shamelessness, immodesty, rascality and deceit' of the priests of the Vishnu temples brought on it an action for libel by the temple authorities. Though Vaishnavite followers were forbidden, under pain of excommunication, to give evidence, a plea of justification was upheld by the Court. The judgment supported the defendant's plea that what is morally wrong cannot be theologically right, and agreed that 'practices which sap the very foundations of morality, if established in the name and under the sanction of religion, ought to be publicly exposed and denounced'. It is not surprising that missionary Wilson, whom the reformers of that time acknowledged as a leader, found in the case evidence that 'educated Brahmins now bid fair to take a leading part in destroying error'. The enlightened Hindu, as a recent Christian expert on Hinduism[1] has told us, has reached the position that every religious usage must submit to the scrutiny of morality and compassion.

Recognition of this fact, combined with the growing realisation that Christ came to fulfil rather than to destroy, accounts for the gradual withdrawal of missionaries from the front ranks of those who urged the need for official action against social and moral abuses. That the later pages of this book lack the personal note which makes the chronicling of the earlier periods so attractive and easy must be ascribed to a praiseworthy desire on the missionaries' part to remain in the background quietly educating public opinion; they encouraged Hindu reformers to set their own house in order by emphasising what was morally great in their religion rather than by

[1] J. N. Farquhar, *Modern religious movements in India.*

frontal attacks on its defects. This policy has been noted recently by the President of the orthodox all-India Hindu Mahasabha,[1] who attributed the lack of measures to reconvert Indian Christians to Hinduism to the Christian missionaries' 'high ground of reasoning and comparative study, leading to toleration and an appreciative understanding of each other's position'. In public affairs they concentrated their explicit and ardent advocacy on reforms that do not run counter to Hinduism or are even in accord with it. In discussion arising out of the government control of opium and liquor traffic they played at times a leading part.

Though the Government during the latter part of our period was assured by a small but steadily growing section of non-Christian reformers that it was not only the right but the duty of the supreme power to intervene where a social custom or religious rite outraged the Indian sense of humanity, or inflicted injustice on helpless classes of the people, the expediency of enforcing this view was frequently called into question and often denied. For every critic who blamed the authorities for refusing to suppress what was contrary to all principles of justice and morality there were always two who represented all such action as interference with religion and an insult to Indian society.

That the fabric of this society was essentially religious was undeniable. It was equally true that most of the evils which non-Christian reformers as well as the conscience of the Christian world condemned were sanctioned and even encouraged by popular and plausible interpretation of Hindu religious principles. There were many who urged that Hinduism must be left to reform itself from within instead of being attacked by a merely destructive alien force. There were others who regarded religious fanaticism as a powerful weapon

[1] 1928 meeting at Jubbulpore. *The Times*, April 9th, 1928.

in the armoury of aggressive nationalism. It was so easy to depict all measures that offended the orthodox as inspired by racial or political selfishness. When we find a prominent nationalist[1] in 1928 introducing a bill in the Indian legislative assembly for the repeal of the 1850 Caste Disabilities Act, which secured all who changed their religion against the loss of civil rights, we realise the connection between political and racial feeling and reactionary orthodoxy. And when in the same year we find nine Brahmins[2] condemned by the Allahabad High Court for murder of another Brahmin, who had tried to improve the condition of the depressed classes in his village, and two Hindus sentenced in Oudh for having aided and abetted the voluntary 'suttee' of a widow, we can understand how easy it must have been throughout the period to meet any proposal for social or moral legislation by a reference to the explosive and pervading forces of Hinduism.

This explains why a Government that had stamped infanticide, suttee, and human sacrifice as crimes, though they were sanctioned by religion, found it so difficult to proceed in a crusade against the other evils bound up with Hinduism, such as child marriage, ill-treatment of widows and 'untouchables', temple prostitution, and the varied manifestations of obscenity and sexual obsession. There was a quickening of the Christian conscience and ever-growing interest at home in Indian affairs. Year by year, as prescribed by the Act of 1858, a report on the moral and material progress of India was submitted to Parliament But at the same time there was an ever-growing feeling of the danger of enacting measures so far in advance of public opinion, taken as a whole, that they could not be enforced, and an ever-growing hope

[1] Mr. Kelkar. *The Times*, 17th March, 1928.

[2] This and the following case were reported by Allahabad correspondent of *The Times*, April 26th, 1928.

that education would steadily swell the ranks of reformers till a stage was reached when legislation would be either effective or unnecessary. Both feelings, of danger and hope alike, were fostered by those who on racial, religious, or purely selfish grounds, resented all attempts at changing Hindu society.

There is no element in Brahminism which is more repugnant to Christian feeling than that which comprehends the marriage laws and customs of Hindu society. Precise teaching of the Shastras on this subject is disputed even among Hindus. But it is generally admitted that for a Brahmin anyhow the postponement of a daughter's marriage until after the age of puberty is a deadly sin, punishable in this life by outcasting, and involving terrible retribution after death. Consummation of marriage as soon as the child bride attains puberty is certainly recommended, if not definitely prescribed, in the Hindu scriptures that are best known and most respected. To what extent Brahmin laws and customs are imposed as a religious duty on inferior castes need not here be discussed. Census reports assure us that there is a tendency on the part of all castes, as they climb the social ladder, to adopt the marriage customs of the Brahmins. It is normal throughout Hindu society for girls to undergo the burden of motherhood within a year of puberty.

The devastating effect of this usage on national physique has often been emphasised. We are here concerned rather with the shock to Christian feelings caused by callous disregard for the health and dignity of helpless girls and by the demoralising effect of early preoccupation with sexual matters. Though this feeling of disgust is shared by all non-Christian reformers in India, and even by many, who for various reasons disapprove of legislative action, their speeches and writings generally emphasise the damage inflicted on the nation at large rather than the claims of the individual. It is to the conscience of the Christian world that the cry of the helpless for justice appeals.

Be that as it may, there has been no lack of urgent appeals to the Government from non-Christian bodies and individuals to deal with this evil. And Indian leaders have been found ready to incur abuse and unpopularity, particularly distasteful to the Indian mind, by introducing or supporting remedial measures. A petition in 1882 was met by advice to wait for the co-operation of the parties most interested. In 1891 an 'Age of consent' bill which made consummation criminal before the girl reached the age of twelve was carried by Government in the teeth of violent opposition. In 1925 the age of consent was raised by statute to thirteen for married girls and fourteen for unmarried. When next the subject came up in 1928 a bill introduced by a private Hindu member[1] aimed at the abolition of child marriage.

To enforce a regulation referring to consummation is difficult. The fact of marriage increases the temptation to break the law and the difficulty of enforcing it.

The bill, as amended in Committee and circulated by Government for opinion, provides pains and penalties for anyone who performs or assists in the marriage of boys and girls of less than eighteen and fourteen years of age respectively, and for any man marrying a girl below this age. The Government in approving the general intention of the measure reserves its final decision till the opinion of the general public is known.

We have pursued the subject beyond the period of this chapter because the discussion evoked by this bill and the similar measures before provincial councils has brought to a head the controversy of the last fifty years. It illustrates the difficulties attending any measure of

[1] Mr. Sardar.

reform which brings Christian and Hindu principles into conflict. For the bill in its present shape seems to some a menace to orthodox Hinduism. Denial for a time of the full privileges of matrimony, which is all that legislation hitherto has attempted, is not direct interference with religious ordinances as generally interpreted and accepted. But the latest proposal forbids the Brahmin hierarchy to perform or assist at the marriage ceremony of girls until they have passed the age limit prescribed by their scriptures. It is on those responsible for the proceedings that the penalty will fall ; evasion of the law will no longer be possible.

The national social conference, and reformers such as Mrs. Besant who are also zealous for the rights and interests of Hinduism, have adopted a sturdy and resolute attitude in support of the measure. Some have in fact gone beyond it in urging that the marriage age for boys and girls should be twenty-one and sixteen respectively, and they have shown in this connection a realisation of the dangers to which boys as well as girls are subjected by the present usage. But some of the argument brought forward by the numerous opponents of the measure are extremely plausible and show that, even if illiterate fanaticism or vested interests are the basis of all opposition, trained intellect and nimble wits are doing their best to obscure this fact. Though the opposition is led by Brahmins, it would be a mistake to suppose either that Brahmins are to be found only among the opponents or that they constitute the whole of the opposition. The Marwaris, for instance, famous in the world of finance and commerce, are as a class in opposition. But they leave arguments to the Brahmins.

To the Christian mind the frequent use of the phrase 'Marriage sacrament' by opponents of the measure is interesting and significant. 'Here', say the critics, 'we have an attempt to break up a religious conception of marriage which underlies Hindu society. It is directed essentially against the Brahmins who have taught from time to time immemorial that marriage before puberty symbolises and perpetuates the complete identification, spiritual as well as physical, of man and wife. For other countries and climates other manners and other laws. For India divine wisdom has ordained the protection of womanhood from temptation and assault, and the assertion of her complete dependence on her husband, by the safeguard of marriage before she reaches an age when such assertive protection becomes an urgent necessity. The abuse of privileges legalised by child marriage may be an admitted evil. But it is not an abuse definitely encouraged by religion (this in actual fact is a subject of dispute), and it will yield to the education of public opinion. In any case it is not comparable to the evils to which unprotected childhood would be exposed in a society which has been taught by legislation to disregard the Shastras and to submit to no kind of religious restraint.'

That such arguments can be advanced, in some cases *bona fide*, by a society smarting under the lash of *Mother India*,[1] to convince a western world dumbfounded by that book, shows at once the subtlety of the Hindu mind and its characteristic indifference to material facts. Facts obtainable from the domestic or social experience of the normal Hindu, or from the statistics and reports to which the 'intelligentsia' have access, do not make such an appeal to minds that find reality in a world of ideas as they do to the western mind. Nothing but Christianity is likely to establish in India a firm connection between the worlds of facts and religious ideas. Pending this connection, and the more rapid growth of a new spirit in India, no legislation, however Christian in principle, can very greatly improve the condition of women in

[1] By Miss Mayo. See p. 233 and list of authorities.

India. But this is no argument against such legislation, nor an admission that 'public opinion' as at present directed in India must be substituted for legal enactments. It is for the Government ultimately to decide what use should at various stages be made of either instrument. But those who at present are most optimistic about public opinion are unfortunately least to be counted on as its leaders.

The question of civil marriage also aroused controversy during the period. Dalhousie's Act of 1856 had legalised the remarriage of Hindu widows. But though the legal rights and status of those contracting such remarriage were safeguarded, it was for obvious reasons difficult for those who remained in the Hindu communion to find anybody both authorised and willing to perform the marriage ceremony. The Brahmo Samaj[1] provided for some a way out of the difficulty. But there were reformers who favoured an extension of the rights of civil marriage, conferred by the Special Marriage Act of 1872 on those who professed none of the religions established in India, to the adherents of these religions. Orthodox opposition was strong. The enforced celibacy of widows, particularly of those bereft of their husbands before they have emerged from childhood, has been responsible for much temptation, much immorality, and a suspicious attitude towards the whole class that is largely responsible for the inhumane treatment which is often their lot, and which makes their employment for educational or social work difficult. On the other hand, no man-made law could set aside the Hindu conception of complete identification of man and wife. The religious objection to widow remarriage was a survival of the idea which underlay suttee.

One of the first measures introduced by a Hindu

[1] A Hindu reform society retaining only a vague connection with Hinduism. 6388 adherents in 1921, mainly in Bengal and Bihar. See Farquhar, *Modern religious movements in India*.

member, Sir H. S. Gour, in the reformed Legislature established by the constitutional changes of 1921, was for the extension of the rights of civil marriage to members of all communities. This was intended to facilitate not only the remarriage of Hindu widows, but also intercaste marriage, without forfeiture of legal rights or status as Hindus, just as, for instance, marriage in an English registry office is legally without prejudice to the contractors' membership of the established Church of England.

The status of caste as a divine ordinance for the restraint of lawless men and the safeguarding of social obligations was, of course, urged as an insuperable objection to intercaste marriage. But the Special Marriage (Amendment) Act of 1923 finally extended civil marriage without loss of rights, except as regards adoption, to all members of the Hindu, Sikh, Jaina and Buddhist religions.

From earliest times the position of the depressed classes, the 'untouchables', in India, has aroused the indignation of the Christian world. During the period under review there was no subject in which the Government could look for a larger measure of support from Hindu reformers inspired by Christian ideas than that of improving the status of these classes. From the time of Keshab Chander Sen to that of Mr. Gandhi there have not been wanting influential Hindus who have not feared to risk their popularity by exposing and trying to remove this cancerous growth from Hindu society. For legislation there has been little scope. The Queen's Proclamation of 1858 established beyond all doubt a determination to secure fair and impartial treatment for every caste and class. The Education Despatch of 1854 opened in theory every school and college to every caste and every outcaste in India. Administrative action has been in accordance with these fundamental principles. It is to the credit of the Madras Government that they took the lead, in the part of India most dominated by caste, not only in trying to enforce these principles, but also in adapting their system to the circumstances of these classes and in holding out special inducements for their education.[1] Consequential progress, educationally and otherwise, has been pitifully meagre. Its acceleration, by universal admission, depends on the extension of Christian settlements and other settlements that are gradually arising on Christian lines, and generally on the spread of a Christian spirit, rather than on administrative action. Though the Government has never refused a hearing to representations of offences against the spirit of its proclamations or regulations, it has never succeeded in the removal of local prejudice. Its officers have often been constrained to overlook acts of gross injustice to which their attention has not officially been drawn. In 1919 the Madras Government admitted that only 609 schools out of 8157 admitted 'untouchables'. The organ of the Servants of India Society in 1921 complained that such admission was limited to only 7 per cent of the schools attended by Hindu pupils. This year the national social conference of India has again protested against the exclusion of these classes from public roads, wells, tanks and rest houses. A recent resolution which committed a provincial legislative council[2] to a policy of pressure on local bodies to secure these public rights for all was clearly regarded as an expression of piety rather than the initiation of an effective campaign.

The present position of the 'Eta',[3] the outcastes of Japan, affords another striking example of the powerlessness of those in authority to help classes condemned by

[1] In 1893.
[2] Bombay.
[3] See report in *The Times*, Dec. 27th, 1927.

social usage, based on religion, in a land where Christian principles are not firmly established.

Christianity is distinguished by its stern repudiation of all connection between things spiritual and things obscene. In alliance with the good taste that is common to the best men of every race and religion, and inspired by the international activities of Geneva, this hatred of obscenity was responsible for an Act in 1923 which made all traffic in objects, books, and pictures, that were obviously and offensively obscene a criminal offence. But all objects that in origin and use are *bona fide* religious are expressly excepted from the operation of the Act. The superficial may be reminded of the light-hearted tolerance with which the Roman Government viewed the follies of subject religions. It is surprising to the western mind, though perhaps characteristic of Hindu orthodoxy, that it was not roused by the condemnation, worthy of a Marcus Aurelius, that was implicit in this exception.

The prostitution of women, which no Christian moralist has ever tried to defend, is definitely associated, in the popular mind anyhow, with certain forms of temple management in India. The national social conference has emphatically condemned the whole Devadasi system ; a private measure directed against it, and aimed generally at the restriction of prostitution, has been introduced in a provincial council, evoking in opposition from some quarters arguments that do more credit to the head than the heart of their originators.

The Act of 1925 which raised the age of consent to fourteen in the case of unmarried girls, mitigated some of the worst evils of the Devadasi system.

There is perhaps no historical justification for associating the humanitarian movement that transformed the Roman empire in the third and fourth centuries and

England in the eighteenth and nineteenth centuries solely or essentially with the doctrines of Christianity. But it is certain that the resolute translation of humanitarian ideas into action was the work essentially of men inspired by the spirit and power of Christ. The Indian Penal Code which after many years of labour came into full force at the beginning of our period brought into the crude and harsh world of Indian criminal procedure some of the humanitarian spirit that marks all the work of Macaulay, Maine, and Fitzjames Stephen. Its refusal to recognise any caste distinction in criminals, though commonplace to India of to-day, is in striking contrast to the Hindu law-giver[1] who distinguished a Brahmin from a Sudra murderer and lightly regarded the stabbing of an outcaste by a highcaste man polluted by his proximity on the high-road.

In the prison system, and still more in the reformatory schools, the disciplinary and formative functions of punishment, as apart from its retributive and deterrent, have for the first time in Indian penal history received practical recognition.

An Act for the prevention of cruelty to animals was passed in 1890, and was applied expressly at a later date to the protection of goats ; with what results may be judged by those who have witnessed the proceedings at Kalighat or weighed the evidence adduced in *Mother India*. Religious scruples and orthodox opposition led to the exemption of cattle and all temple precincts from the operation of an Act passed by the Bombay Government recently for the destruction of aged, wounded, and diseased animals.

In 1812 William Carey saw a leper burned to death and heard a Brahmin convert admit that he had once helped to bury a leper alive. Before our period ends

[1] The Laws of Manu ; dating from about 900 B.C., and providing the foundation of Hindu law.

the Government was entrusting funds to Christian missions for the maintenance of leper hospitals and to its medical department for investigating the causes of this fell disease.

EPILOGUE
THINGS PRESENT AND TO COME

EPILOGUE

THINGS PRESENT AND TO COME

Recent verdicts on British government in India—its moral and social achievements—and debt to missions—influence on public opinion—and religions in India—the coming constitutional changes—and probable effect on the tone of government—anti-Christian measures improbable—no reaction, but lack of vigour and motive power to be expected—cardinal defects in Hinduism—strength and weakness of Mr. Gandhi—need of a dynamic religion with historical basis—Mohammedan conservatism—and educational backwardness—no Christian arguments against extension of self-government—a question of expediency, not religion—spiritual concentration the Churches' task—and aloofness from political parties and government—the position of Indian Christians—no claim to special political privileges—separate representation undesirable—need for keeping in touch with depressed classes—political and social importance of depressed classes—possibilities of Christian work in India—the call to service.

A SCHOLAR reviewing in the *Cambridge Modern History*[1] the work of the British Government in India up to 1910 records 'a consistent and sustained attempt to justify on high political and ethical grounds the existence of our Empire'. This verdict, the impartiality of which need not be questioned, on its ethical side is supported by a more recent writer whose nationality frees her from suspicion of bias, and whose moral fervour and desire to ascertain the truth stand out in every page. Miss Mayo, in *Mother India*, acquits the British Government of all responsibility for the social and moral evils of India with which she is mainly concerned. Such moral progress as she finds time and inclination to admit, and most of the attempts at progress, which are less grudg-

[1] Vol. xii, p. 499.

ingly recorded, are associated unequivocally, though not solely, with the supreme authority in India.

It was the intention of this book to examine rather than to defend the ethical tendencies of our work in India. But consideration of the facts that such examination has brought into prominence has convinced the writer of the justice of these conclusions. It has led him on to the further conclusion that our government of India has earned the title of Christian by the character of its activities, which have progressively displayed qualities emphasised by the Christian faith, and still more by the essentially Christian vigour and hopefulness that have inspired them.

Clearly, if the facts gleaned in this book are accepted, the Government of India by 1920 had moved a long way in the Christian direction from the pitiful condition that called for its chastisement by Burke. Sixty years after a British Parliament in 1784 had made the East India Company a trustee for the welfare of India a Christian-spirited servant of the Company found in its rule 'an utter want of nobleness'; 'marks of its commercial origin', a secular concentration on 'protection of life and property and revenue collection', 'a distaste for abstract ideas and an absence of serious insight into life'. But the author of *Oakfield*[1] admitted also that the 'lower good', which the Company mistook for a higher, was in fact 'higher than the highest of most other Governments'; its practice, as distinguished from its principles, was far more just and liberal. Even as he wrote, the extra 'shiploads of courage' and 'bushels of pure unselfish enthusiasm' for which he indented had been embarked. Lawrence and Dalhousie were ready to receive the torch lit by Wellesley and Bentinck and to hand it on to Curzon.

It was not only the faith that was in them, but also

[1] See p. 140.

the steady and constant reminder of that faith, applied by Christian agencies in India, that kept moral and social aims before the eyes of Governors and their Councils. It was the considered opinion of a Parliamentary committee in 1837 that 'the intercourse of Europeans has been, unless when attended by missionary exertion, a source of many calamities to less civilised nations. Sir Harry Johnstone,[1] though not theologically on the side of the angels, declared many years later, from the experience of his African administration, that in all questions of forced labour, liquor, and land, it was the missionary who had stood between the natives and exploitation. Not necessarily by political or economic intervention, in no way by interfering in other peoples' business, but by spiritual teaching and example the missions in India were as useful in reminding Christian rulers of their faith as in communicating it to their subjects.

To this stimulus and support of Christian effort was added before long a subsidiary force created by that effort. The best minds in the Indian and non-Christian world were gradually enlisted in the fight against social evils. The predominance of Christian ethics and statecraft is shown theoretically in the manifestos and programmes of many Indian states and social reform federations. It has borne fruit in the administration of some Indian states and in the support given to Government, and initiative taken, in much of its social legislation.

In adapting to Indian civilisation moral and social ideas historically associated with the west the Government has tried to develop everything indigenous that is informed by a similar spirit or is capable of assimilation to it. After long years of hesitation, due partly to selfish

[1] Geographer and African administrator. Quoted by Ogilvie in *Our Empire's debt to Missions.*

fear and partly to a disinterested and sincere belief that the preservation of an Empire on which the very existence of society depended demanded an assumption of religious indifference, it passed from an indifferent neutrality to an open profession of its faith. Claiming no monopoly in high ideals for western civilisation or for Christianity, it gave convincing proof of its intention to protect all religious rites and doctrines that were not dangerous to society. Macaulay said rightly that 'by using our official power to make proselytes we should have produced the dissolution of society'.[1] It is equally true that by using the power that Christianity gave us to protect and strengthen society we have made proselytes. Hinduism, as Sir Alfred Lyall pointed out, has been led by its experience of our benevolent and powerful aristocracy to include in its catholic theology the idea of a divine providence shaping the happiness of men.[2] The lives and examples of many servants of Government have contributed to the more positive success of Christian missions.

When we turn from the intention and methods of the British Government to its actual results, humility and misgivings take the place of exaltation. India in 1920 was perhaps as far removed from a Christian country of that date as from the India of 1784. If we compare, not the greatest nor the worst, but the average members of India and European society, and study their respective attitudes towards their social inferiors, the economically depressed, or women, if we consider their practical recognition of the rights of other men and their duty towards their neighbours, we shall have good cause to congratulate, not ourselves indeed, but the force that vitalises European society.

The constitutional changes of 1920 transferred a large measure of power to men and bodies that are not

[1] *Essay on Church and State.* [2] *Asiatic Studies.*

essentially associated and impregnated with the Christian ideals, principles, and vigour, that animated the autocratic system which came to an end then. Though the supreme Government of India on its executive side is still composed of men selected by those who disseminated the old system, and inspired, we may assume, by their spirit, its policy, and more particularly its legislation, is shaped by an Assembly and Council of State in which elected members can outvote the official and nominated elements. In the provinces the departments which are most concerned with the social and moral development are controlled by ministers responsible to councils which represent an electorate not essentially Christian in energy or feeling. It would be rash to assume that the further changes now under consideration will reduce what one may without offence call the non-Christian factor in the Government. It is far more likely to increase it.

There is not the smallest reason to anticipate any antagonism to Christian mission work or interference with their work as an outcome of these constitutional changes. Neither the history of the last half-century nor the events of the last eight years suggest it. Though racial bitterness may remain and even grow, the Indian Christian has established his position in Indian society. Thanks largely to his firmness and the wisdom of our missionaries Christianity is no longer viewed as a western and exotic plant.

Nor is there any likelihood of ideals, in which Christians and the finer products of Hinduism and Islam find a meeting ground, losing their hold on India. Many will agree with Mr. Edward Thompson that in parts of India where Brahminical or Rajput influence is strong the withdrawal of British rule might lead to local outbreaks of suttee.[1] But they would also agree with him

[1] *Suttee—a historical and philosophical enquiry.* Allen & Unwin, 1927.

that it would not again be established as a universal custom. Against this, as against the revival of other evils that British rule has completely or nearly suppressed, public opinion based on ideas that have taken hold of the leaders of Indian thought and feeling would be too strong. And sensitiveness to external criticism would be too keen. It is hard to suppress a social usage in India. But it is not easy to restore it to a society that has been accustomed throughout the ages to change gradually, and not to regret what has been given up.

But it is hard to believe that there will be no falling off in the pace of moral and social reform, which indeed has never been distinguished by its speed in India. There is even a danger of the possibility of such reform, so far as Government's share in it is concerned, being forgotten. Ideas by themselves have never raised a nation nor initiated reform. Paul could do for the Roman Empire what Seneca the Stoic, with all the lofty idealism of his school, wholly failed to do. For he had not only the ideas of Seneca, but a living force within him. Is it too pessimistic to imagine an India in which the spiritually minded reformers, who have been ready to support the British Government, will be as powerless to stir an Indian Government as the Stoics were to dispel the social inertia of the Roman Empire? Of courage there will be no lack. But will it go beyond boldness of speech and writing? What may be found wanting is the hopefulness and energy, the faith that is idealism in action, the frank recognition of facts, and the insight into reality, that characterise the really Christian attitude towards life.

To some the character and career of Mr. Gandhi might seem to dispel this fear. Here is a man who has extracted from Hinduism what is morally and spiritually best, who has shown himself fearless before the official world and reactionary Hinduism in the practical expression of his faith, and who has carried, if it be possible, the Christian virtue of hopefulness to excess in his confidence that he would be able to restrain the superstitious and illiterate masses that he was trying to rouse. Professing to find in the Christian gospel much that strengthens and sustains what he learned from Hindu teachers, he has always attributed his power to the Bhagvad Gita rather than to the Sermon on the Mount, and he notes much that is spiritually and morally lacking even in the highest type of Christian life and teaching in India to-day. Is it not reasonable to see in him the type of great and influential teacher that Hinduism can produce, and to expect that from among the millions who look to him as their prophet at least some will rise to claim and use the prophet's mantle?

Mr. Gandhi's spiritual hold on men's hearts and wills has undoubtedly been due to his resolute application of great principles which, whatever may have been their avowed origin in him, are essentially connected with Christ. Accepting religion as the supreme guide and only source of power in all walks of life, he has shown by his own example the efficacy of prayer, ascetic and soul compelling suffering, and love. He has come near to convincing millions that by voluntary suffering alone a man may fit himself to rule and triumph over the powers of darkness. And he has done more than any non-Christian perhaps since Buddha to show India that true religion is not a means of propitiating gods with a view to material prosperity, or of obtaining sanction for a mode of life, but a source of moral strength and spiritual regeneration.

But his frequent failure in the world of action, which he has been far too honest not to admit, has been due to a defect from which the genuine Christian prays daily to be freed, and of which the highest type of Hindu mind seems seldom to be conscious. The Christian prays 'for a right judgment in all things' and is conscious that the spirit of Christ alone will keep before him the importance, and give him the capacity, of facing and interpreting correctly the facts of the world in which he may play his part. Christ was 'the truth' as well as the way and the life. Neither he nor Paul ever showed any lack of insight into the facts of the Roman Empire and Jewish world in which their lot was cast. It was this insight that preserved them from the appalling blunders of Mr. Gandhi.

The Brahmin also prays to the light of the Universe, that it may illumine his understanding. But the world that is to be illuminated is that of ideas rather than that of facts. And the connection between the two worlds is not, as it was for Christ or Paul, vital. One who knows the Hindu student well reports that it is natural for him to ask whether a lunar landscape viewed through a telescope is real, and whether Alice in Wonderland is true.[1] It would also be natural for him to await the answers with indifference. Mr. Gandhi places truth with courage in his list of essential virtues. He is clearly incapable of deliberate falsehood. But the truth which he appreciates is that of idea, and his truthful action is that which is in accordance with a strongly preconceived idea. He has never shown any ability, nor, one might almost add, any desire, to test his ideas in the light of actual facts or to adapt his action to circumstances as revealed by history or science.

This indifference to facts is what led his English judge,[2] after paying generous tribute to his idealism, to add that he could not conceive how he had failed to foresee the inevitable consequences of his appeal to the illiterate masses. These consequences included riot and brutal murder. Even more appalling, because more

[1] *India in Conflict,* Young and Ferrers.

[2] Before passing sentence at the close of Mr. Gandhi's trial for sedition at Ahmedabad, 1921.

permanent, have been the results of his misreading of history. In preaching the spiritual degradation, the complete demoralisation, of India brought about by British rule, he has accentuated racial bitterness at a time when only friendly co-operation could remove the obstacles to constitutional progress. Yet no one with a firm determination to use even a superficial knowledge of history or current affairs could possibly have thought that the India of 1920 was spiritually or morally worse than the India of 1784, or denied that our rule had been on the whole stimulating.

There is no time or need to emphasise other errors of judgment, as for instance his misreading of the Khilafat movement or of modern economic tendencies. Let us concentrate on the simplest and most striking examples. Mr. Gandhi's cardinal ideas were irreproachable. Of those facts which claimed attention in a mind saturated with such ideas he took cognisance. The rest, not wilfully but characteristically, he ignored. Certain actions of the British Government seemed to him, perhaps rightly, inconsistent with justice or generosity. Therefore the Government as a whole was spiritually condemned. Certain officials or clients of the Government showed a disposition to gain their favour by subservience. Therefore it was responsible for 'Slave mentality'. Suffering is elevating. Therefore an attitude towards Government which involves such suffering is to be approved, whatever its effect on the Government, or the peace and order of the country, may be.

Christ's abstention from any kind of political or racial teaching may have been due to his preoccupation with spiritual values. But such preoccupation never dulled his insight into the characters and lives of individuals and races with whom he came into contact, nor did it make him reluctant to admit the weakness of his disciples and to shape his course accordingly. Paul was intimately acquainted with all the details and principles of Roman administration. If he saw its faults he realised also that it was 'ordained of God', as a civilising agency and a means whereby the great idea for which he stood could be propagated. The greatest saints of Christian history have shown a similar capacity for studying and understanding facts. Mr. Gandhi in this particular is not among the saints.

His intellectual 'sloppiness' may perhaps be traced ultimately to the same cardinal defect of Hinduism as the lack of will power and driving force which has also been suggested as a possible cause of failure in a non-Christian India. Hinduism does not rest on a historical basis. It has no foundation in facts. Many of its gods, and the supreme God towards which it has always been groping its way, are to the best of their followers a personification of lofty ideals. They inspire a feeling of Bhakti, a desire for personal disinterested service. But they create no sense of reality, moving as they do in a dim world of ideas. They are not themselves incarnate in the hearts of men as a historical fact. Through poets such as Tukaram, Kabir, or Tagore,[1] they can speak to men. But they do not leave the realm of poetry or inspire hopeful action. Till India realises as a historical fact that the fullness of divine power in man was actually manifest in Christ, and that this power has been perpetuated in history by His spirit, the work of its most exalted minds will resemble, in its intellectual foundations, a house builded on sand or, in its moral force, a machine admirably planned and constructed but without fuel. Christianity alone, as Pascal realised, exalts without puffing up and humiliates without abasing. Its history shows the importance of humble-minded attention to facts and the infinite capacity of the inspired soul for progress.

[1] Rabindranath Tagore; poet, philosopher, novelist and educationalist. See list of authorities.

Islam in India may yet do more for the social and moral progress of her peoples than Hinduism. If it has not during the last half-century produced so many leading advocates of reform, even in proportion to the number of its adherents, this may be attributed to educational backwardness rather than to the character of its faith. It may not in its highest manifestations rise to quite the same level as Hinduism at its best. But it certainly does not sanction so many social evils or present so many obstacles to progress. Fundamentally different in all respects, it possesses a virility and hopefulness that have made it in past ages a civilising agency in varied localities and at the present time a force to be taken into account in Africa. Its potential value, compared with that of Christianity, depends largely on its ability to develop a dynamic view of religion. So long as it is bound by the letter of a scripture intended for a primitive people in a primitive age, its zeal for reform, however powerful it may be, will be restricted in scope. For some time past its leading men have been moving in the direction of a theory of doctrinal development. How far this is carried and applied to social affairs must depend on Islamic contact with Christian thought and action.

If a bolder development of self-government in India means a further surrender of power to bodies and persons not animated to the same extent as the old autocratic regime by definitely Christian principles, it may legitimately be asked whether such development is from the Christian point of view acceptable. Even those who, with justice, anticipate no reversion to anti-Christian usages already suppressed or abandoned may ask whether as trustees we are entitled to give privileges that may slacken the pace of reform and postpone the recognition of the rights of women and the depressed classes. A protest successfully made by the Church Missionary Society in Uganda against the abandonment of that country by the British East African Company might by some be quoted in this connection.[1]

The conditions in Uganda were quite different. Education and other civilising agencies were not so firmly established; there was nothing equivalent in social stability to Hindu society. The mission which had preceded the European political agency had acted as intermediary between the rulers and the ruled and had taught the natives to look to it for political guidance and protection. In countenancing the withdrawal of English rule it would have betrayed a trust.

In the case of India a protest on distinctively Christian lines would certainly be inexpedient, and in the opinion of many impossible. Give any man or nation its deserts and who would escape servitude? There is no European country where the rights of the weak and depressed might not better be safeguarded by a Christian autocrat than they are by existing forms of government. But development on these lines is not in accordance with the Christian spirit. The only theological explanation of free will is that omnipotent God allows men the possibility of doing wrong because without it there is no possibility of their becoming good. The Christian does not 'apply' this idea to politics, or associate his religion essentially with political democracy or anti-Imperialism, because he knows the dangers of political entanglement and realises that in the complex world of politics there is much good and much evil in every party. But though study of both sides of a question may lead him to vote for an Imperialist, he will never on essentially religious grounds oppose an extension of freedom. Whether India has learned enough to avoid liberty degenerating into licence, and whether with larger powers she will be able to raise the weak and lift

[1] A British Protectorate was established in 1894.

up the feeble heart, are questions on which Christians do and will differ. They will also differ as to whether the risk of inflicting suffering on the weak is so great as to be undesirable. But as Christians they can never say that all risk is to be avoided. Such a contention would condemn the attitude of almost every Christian father to his sons and the amazing venture on which the Father of us all embarked.

Nor is it likely, if we may judge from the spirit of the recent mission conference at Jerusalem,[1] that Christian bodies will raise the question of guarantees, or demand the insertion in a charter of self-government of a clause safeguarding the work of missions or protecting the Christian religion. Under Article 22 of the League of Nations all mandatory powers are responsible for the prohibition of abuses, such as the slave trade or arms and liquor traffic. If in accordance with such a spirit a self-governing India were to be expressly charged with the responsibility for suppressing whatever is offensive to civilised humanity, the Christian world would rejoice. And if, following the precedent of the conditions imposed when the Congo river[2] was entrusted to Leopold of Belgium, the British Government were to insist on a fair field for all religions including the Christian, missions might be ready to claim protection under such a clause, if it were without detriment to spiritual work or status. But it is for Government to offer, not for missions to demand, this measure of support.

Christian bodies have come to recognise that 'moral or spiritual obligations convey no civil or legal right' and that the Christian as such can claim no special rights. In the India of the future it is particularly inexpedient that Christianity should be associated with

[1] Easter, 1928. See list of authorities.

[2] In 1885.

political controversy, or that it should rely on any Government, least of all on an alien or western Government. That it will meet with persecution or even antagonism is very doubtful. Such persecution, if it ever came, could appropriately be met only by wider exercise of the Christian virtues and more convincing proof of their services to India.

It will be easier for missions, under a more Indian form of Government, to disentangle themselves from the official and political world. They will better be able to assert the essential difference between the spheres and methods of Government and those of the Christian churches. The churches are concerned with spiritual values and their influence on the nature of men. No political change that leaves that nature as it is will seriously concern them.

Increasingly they will be able to insist on man's eternal life in God, leaving to other bodies the regulation of man's material life on earth, but trusting that their influence will ultimately be felt in such regulations. They may hope that some time in the far distant future the kingdom of Heaven will develop in India as a civilised society marked by justice and material prosperity. But the coming of this time will be retarded, not advanced, if they confuse a possible result with an immediate and imperative duty. The more British authority is withdrawn from India, the greater the responsibility of Christian missions for upholding Christian principles in the administration of the country. This they can do not by identifying themselves with any particular measures or parties, but by acting as a spiritual power house, from which ultimately all the force required for initiating and carrying through reforms must be derived.

An essential feature of such a 'power house' will be a Christian system of education, recognised by the State, but aided by it only if such aid is compatible with complete freedom, and if it involves no risk of identification with a secular Government system. There is no chance of the development in India of any state system that will recognise adequately the educational importance of religion. The situation is widely different from that in England, where the general acceptance of Christianity, and the absence of any religious feeling similar to that which separates Hinduism from Islam, makes Bible instruction possible as a real and integral part of the curriculum. So long as all examinations in India are controlled directly or indirectly by the Government there will be an unreality in religious education even in mission schools. Only by schools and colleges where religious instruction can come into its own will the inadequacy and comparative failure of secular education, which is already suspected, be made quite clear, and the real possibilities of education be exposed.

Whether the great body of Indian Christians in India will be able, as a body, to keep clear of political entanglement has yet to be seen. Fortunately there is no need to remind it of the dangers of denationalisation. All its leaders are determined to play their part as Indians, not as offshoots of a western and alien religion, in the salvation of India. Very properly they are politically showing more concern in the welfare of India than in the position of Christians. At a time like the present it is inevitable that the question of political representation should be considered. It is greatly to the credit of the Indian Christian Conference[1] that it has rejected the idea of communal representation, either by election or, what would be still more dangerous, by government nomination. Christians have no political privileges to maintain. Their duty of influencing public opinion can be fulfilled in many ways, other than that of actual

[1] See report of All India Christian Conference, Dec., 1927. There have however been further developments since this was written.

participation in the work of Government. It is doubtful whether they are wise in demanding the reservation of seats for Christians elected by a joint electorate. But this demand perhaps represents a desire to fall in with the reasonable demands of other religions and the proposals of the liberal federation rather than a wish to secure or safeguard any political advantages. Particularly encouraging in the present crisis is a movement directed against political or social separation of Christians of pariah origin from the depressed classes who have not yet found a way out of their misery. As a memorial recently presented to the Simon Commission admirably puts it : 'Christianity represents a religious spirit. . . . It is a life dominated by the love of Christ, it is a life of continuous sacrifice of one's dignity, wealth, and health for the sake of others. It never made an Englishman a Scotchman or vice versa. It does not in India confer a new skin or a new bone nor does it make its adherents into a separate caste'.[1] Wise words which might well be adopted as a guiding principle of the whole Christian community in India.

It is not Indian Christians alone who are 'the hope of India', but all who share their desire for India's real welfare and possess the wisdom and energy to work for this desire. It is certainly not to the Brahmins, nor castes that come closest to them, that we shall look entirely or even first for future leaders of social and moral reform, as we looked for administrative and professional help in the earlier days of British rule. As might be expected from their educational pre-eminence they have supplied from their ranks reformers who do credit to their caste. But as a class they are naturally conservative and tenacious. It is to the 'have-nots' that anxious eyes will turn. That 'have-nots' when in office develop

[1] By the Sambhavar Maha Jana Sambhan—an association of Christians of low caste origin.

characteristics similar to those of the 'haves', unless inspired by widely different motives, is to be expected; it was, in the opinion of some, the actual result of the recent non-Brahmin administration in Madras.[1] But help may be expected from all castes and classes rightly informed and inspired, and pre-eminently from the Indian Christians and the outcastes, now depressed by their own failings and the contemptuous neglect and ill-treatment of the Hindu world, but coming steadily and in places rapidly to the front, through the saving grace of Christianity. In physique they are far superior to the Brahmins and they are increasing at a faster rate. In south India even those who have not yet come directly under Christian influence, becoming conscious of their rights and potential value, are beginning to organise themselves in order to assert their position in an Indian world. The movement is perhaps one of the most important and far-reaching results of Christian influence in India. It is not for the Christian evangelist as such to lead or organise any agitation for political rights. But it is clearly the duty of their congregations to keep in the closest and most sympathetic touch with all such movements, and to remember that Christianity never separates class from class, or shows anything but sympathy with those who strive for enlightenment and a share of responsibility.

It is to be hoped also that those who are shaping the constitutional future of India will remember the present weakness and the potential strength of these depressed millions and the comparative advantages of democratic and autocratic modes of Government. It is not enough to consider which form of constitution has in the past been most natural and congenial to India. Looking

[1] The first Government formed under the Constitution of 1920 in Madras was composed of members of the 'Justice' party, so called from the organ of the non-Brahmin party.

to the future also constitution makers must consider the surest way of enlisting the largest measure of active interest and co-operation in the moral and social advancement of India. If they do this they can hardly fail to see the significance or to take into account the potential vigour of millions who are likely during the next half-century to be moulded by Christian influence into useful and progressive citizens.

'Then shall the lame man leap as an hart and the dumb man sing for joy. For in the wilderness shall waters gush out and streams in the desert.' These words are recorded on a fountain which commemorates at Lyallpur the fertilisation of millions of acres of Punjab desert by the government engineers. Great as that work appears to anyone who has surveyed the miles of wheat fields and the smiling villages that surround the fountain, it is a small thing compared with the effect of the British Government and Christian missions on the soil of Indian thought and feeling and social life. Through these agencies, and the spirit that inspired them, have come the ideas that are fertilising that soil, and the power, like that of the sun and the rain, which swells the seed. Whatever form the future Government of India and Indian Christianity may take, it is certain that Englishmen will be ready to give such help as India may require. And India will never reject what is offered in a friendly and Christian spirit. Such helpers, if they bear in mind the record of a Christian Government in India, will not find it hard to follow the advice of one of the greatest of its representatives,[1] 'never to let your enthusiasm be soured or your courage grow dim', but to remember 'that the Almighty has placed your hand on the greatest of His ploughs. To drive the blade a little forward in your time, and to feel that somewhere among the millions you have left a little

[1] Quoted from the *Life of Lord Curzon*, Ronaldshay, vol. 2.

justice or happiness or prosperity, a sense of manliness or moral dignity, a spring of patriotism, a dawn of intellectual enlightenment, or a stirring of duty where it did not exist before—that is enough, that is the Englishman's justification in India'.

BOOKS CONSULTED

GENERAL

Burke, Edmund. Speeches on India (in Works).

Cambridge Modern History. Cambridge University Press.

Creighton, Louise. *Rise and Development of Missions*. Williams and Norgate. [1912].

Educational Records of the Government of India. Calcutta. 1920–22.

Frere, Sir H. Bartle. *Indian Missions*. 3rd edition. 1874.

Rulers of India Series. Clarendon Press. v.d.

Smith, George. *Conversion of India*. Murray. 1893.

Smith, Vincent A. *Oxford Student's History of India*. Clarendon Press. 1919.

Somervell, D. C. *A short History of our Religion*. Bell. 1923.

Stock, Eugene. *History of the Church Missionary Society*. 4 vols. C.M.S. 1899–1916.[1]

PART I

Anderson, P. *The English in West India*. Smith, Elder. 1856.

Buchanan, C. *Apology for Christianity in India*. London. 1813.

Inquisition in Goa, The. Longmans. 1812.

PARTS I AND II

Allen and McClure. *History of the S.P.C.K*. S.P.C.K. 1898.

Buchanan, C. *Apology for promotion of Christianity in India*. 1813.

[1] I wish to record my special debt to this particularly valuable and comprehensive record, without which this book could not have been written.

BOOKS CONSULTED

Buchanan, C. *Life and Letters of.* By H. N. Pearson. Oxford. 1817.

Dubois, J. A. *Hindu Manners, Customs and Ceremonies.* Clarendon Press. 1906.

Dubois, J. A. *Letters on the State of Christianity in India.* Longmans. 1823.

Fenger, J. F. *History of the Tranquebar Mission.* Madras. 1906.

*Hobhouse, Walter. *The Church and the World in India and History.* Macmillan. 1910.

Papers relating to East Indian Affairs. London. 1813.

Pascoe, C. F. *Two Hundred Years of the S.P.G.* S.P.G. 1901.

Penny, F. *The Church in Madras.* Smith, Elder. 1904.

Schwartz of Tanjore. By J. Page. S.P.C.K. 1921.

Select Committee of the House of Commons on Affairs of the East India Company. London. 1812.

Smith, Sydney. A Memoir by Lady Holland. Longmans. 1869.

Wilberforce, William. *Life and Letters*, by his sons. Murray. 1838.

Wilberforce. By R. Coupland. Clarendon Press. 1923.

PARTS I, II AND III

Carey, William. By S. Pearce Carey. Hodder and Stoughton. [1923.]

Carey, William. By F. Deaville Walker. Student Christian Movement. 1926.

Kaye, Sir J. W. *Christianity in India.* Smith, Elder. 1859.

Smith, George. *Twelve Indian Statesmen.* Murray. 1897.

* The quotation from Peile's *Reproach of the Gospels* on p. 53 is taken from this work.

CHRISTIANITY AND GOVERNMENT OF INDIA

PART II

Martyn, Henry. By C. E. Padwick. Student Christian Movement. 1923.

Roebuck, Thomas. *Annals of the College of Fort William*. Calcutta. 1819.

PART III

Aitchison, Sir C. U. *Collection of Treaties, Engagements, etc.* Vol. ii. 1876.

Arnold, W. D. *Oakfield*. Longmans. 1853.

Dalhousie, Marquis of. By Sir W. Lee Warner. Macmillan. 1904.

Duff, Alexander. By George Smith. Hodder and Stoughton. 1879.

Eden's Letters (Miss). Macmillan. 1919.

Hare, David. Biographical Sketch, by P. C. Mitra. Calcutta. 1877.

Heber, Reginald. *Journeys through India*. Murray. 1829.

Holmes, T. Rice E. *History of the Indian Mutiny*. Macmillan. 1913.

Lawrence, Lord, Life of. By R. Bosworth Smith. Smith, Elder. 1883.

Macaulay, T. B., Lord. Life and Letters. by G. O. Trevelyan. Longmans. 1838.

Maclear, G. F. *The Christian Statesman and our Indian Empire*. Cambridge. 1859.

Mozley, J. B. *Essays historical and theological*. Rivingtons. 1878.

Papers relating to Select Committee of the House of Commons on Affairs of the East India Company. 1833 and 1853.

Sherwood, Mary. *Little Henry and his Bearer*. Various editions.

Sleeman.

Thompson, E. J. *Suttee.* Allen and Unwin. 1928.

Trevelyan, C. E. *On the Education of the Indian People.* Longmans. 1838.

Wilkinson, Michael. *Sketches of Christianity in North India.* Seeley. 1844.

Wilson, Daniel. By Josiah Bateman. Murray. 1860.

Wilson, John. By George Smith. Murray. 1878.

PART IV

Andrews, C. F. *The Indian Problem.* Natesan, Madras. n.d.

Farquhar, J. N. *Modern Religious Movements in India.* Macmillan Co. 1915.

**Gandhi.* By R. M. Gray and M. C. Parekh. Student Christian Movement. 1924.

Lyall, Alfred. *Asiatic Studies.* Murray. 1907.

Mayo, Katherine. *Mother India.* Cape. 1928.

Moral and Material Progress of India : Annual Reports of Government of India.

Ogilvie, J. N. *Our Empire's debts to Missions.* Hodder and Stoughton. [1924.]

Report of Edinburgh World Mission Conference. 1910.

Report of Jerusalem International Mission Conference. 1928.

Tagore, Rabindranath. By E. J. Thompson. Oxford University Press. 1921.

Young, F. N. F. and A. Ferrers. *India in Conflict.* S.P.C.K. 1920.

* The quotations on p. 205 are taken from this valuable study.

INDEX

INDEX